I0191962

REGGAE ROADBLOCKS

A MUSIC BUSINESS DEVELOPMENT PERSPECTIVE

LLOYD STANBURY

ABENG PRESS

Copyright © 2015, Lloyd Stanbury

Abeng Press print edition 2015

All rights reserved. No part of this book may be reproduced or transmitted in any form or by any means, electronic or mechanical, including photocopying, recording, or by any information storage retrieval system without the prior written consent of the publisher. Usage without permission is an infringement of the copyright law.

Abeng Press and colophon are trademarks.

National Library of Canada Cataloging in Publication

Stanbury, Lloyd

Reggae Roadblocks - A Music Business Development Perspective

ISBN 978-0-9867253-7-1

1. Music-Business Aspects 2. Music-Genres & Styles-Reggae 3. Business & Economics-Industries-Entertainment.

Book design by Abeng Press

Cover design by Beresford Nicholson

Published in Canada by

Abeng Press

www.AbengPress.com

Contents

Foreword

REGGAE ROADBLOCKS discusses key issues that have affected the development of the business of Jamaican Reggae at both the national and international levels. The issues raised reflect the perspective of the author, Lloyd Stanbury, from his vantage point as a Jamaican music business professional with substantial international industry experience. The cultural and political environment that gave birth to, and affect the development of Reggae music is examined, as well as the attitudes of local music practitioners to international music business structures, norms and trends. Particular emphasis is placed on the impact of Rastafari on the development and global marketing of Reggae music.

REGGAE ROADBLOCKS is targeted at persons directly and indirectly involved in the business of Reggae at the creative and representational levels, as well as the ordinary Reggae music fan. It also provides very interesting and informative reading for students, academics, and policy makers with interests in music industry development from a developing country perspective, in an era of increased globalization and digitization.

The issues highlighted are based on the experiences of the author in his activities as an entertainment attorney and music business consultant, and are gathered from his work over three decades in Jamaica, the Caribbean, Africa, Latin America, North America, Europe and Asia. As a music industry professional, Lloyd Stanbury has functioned as attorney, artist manager, music producer, business consultant, event promoter, lecturer, researcher, media executive, and writer. He has worked with, represented, and met a wide range of creative and business practitioners in Reggae, who operate at both the local and international levels.

Despite the ground-breaking accomplishments of international music superstar Bob Marley, and the successes of other Jamaican artists such as Peter Tosh, Jimmy Cliff, Shaggy and Sean Paul, there is the widely held view among Reggae fans globally that the business of Reggae has struggled to provide commensurate economic and social benefits to Jamaicans.

REGGAE ROADBLOCKS discusses Reggae as a business, and the Jamaican music industry as a contributor to economic and social development. It is the desire of the author to initiate dialogue that will lead to the formulation of new strategies and solutions to grow a structured domestic Jamaican and international Reggae music industry.

Lloyd Stanbury's comments and observations are of global relevance, as they relate to the practice of the business of music within the mainstream international markets, as well as within the domestic and regional markets of the developing countries where Reggae comes from. It is a book that everyone working in and interested in the Reggae music industry should read and reference for greater understanding and development.

Barbara Makeda Blake Hannah
Jamaica Media Productions

Acknowledgements

This book would not be possible without my having had the opportunity to work with the talented artists and music producers I have been associated with since my introduction to the business of Jamaican music in the early 1980s.

To Sly Dunbar and Robbie Shakespeare, much respect is due. Thanks for trusting in me to be the producer and promoter of your Taxi Connection 10th anniversary celebration concert in Kingston in 1983. This was my first lesson in the business of music, and opened the doors that have made this book possible.

To my immediate family, and wife Janet Stanbury, your unconditional love, support and understanding is the fuel that kept me going on this journey, which has been exciting and sometimes frustrating at the same time. Janet, this was your idea, and I am glad I followed your suggestion to write a book.

The readers of my commentaries on Facebook, in magazines and newspapers over the years have been a great source of inspiration and encouragement. Thanks for the comments, both negative and positive. I am also very grateful to those of you in the music industry who took the time out of your busy schedules to make yourselves available for interviews that are included in Reggae Roadblocks. Your perspectives have contributed a great deal to the conversation.

Thank you Beverly "Sista Irie" Shaw for providing your great photos, for conducting interviews, and for the reminders. Thanks also to those persons who have allowed me to use their photo images. Barbara Blake Hannah, give thanks for the time dedicated to editing and formatting advice. Greatly appreciated.

To my first born son Rohan, this is dedicated to you.

Introduction

This book is an effort to highlight and clarify some of the peculiarities of Jamaica's position in the world as a small island nation with a culture, music and talented people whose influence has wide global impact.

Over the past two decades researchers, international organizations, and government agencies in Jamaica have dedicated time and financial resources to studies, training workshops, and other projects aimed at facilitating further development of the business of Reggae music on a national and international scale. These activities have no doubt contributed to increased curiosity with regard to the global economic potential of Reggae. The studies, training workshops, and other related projects have also served to highlight many of the challenges faced by music industry operators in Jamaica, as well as their international trading partners, as they seek to collaborate to expand and service the global demand for Reggae music.

The number of persons seeking to get involved in the business of Reggae as creative, technical, management and support service providers, has increased over the years. This increased level of interest is not only evident inside Jamaica, but also within the developing markets of the Caribbean, Latin America and Africa, as well as the major music markets of North America and Western Europe. The annual Rototom Reggae Contests for live band performances, have reported figures of 256 entrants from 11 countries in Latin America,[1] and 208 participants from 28 countries in Europe.[2] Concurrently with this increased interest and the international successes of some Jamaican artists, fans and industry practitioners have expressed concern about the level of business development support coming from government and private investors inside Jamaica. Complaints by artists about exploitation and discrimination are also still frequently heard.

In recent years several show promoters and distributors of Jamaican Reggae music in North America, have either reduced the level of their operations, gone out of business, or shifted focus to non-Jamaican Reggae. Many who remain in business speak constantly of the challenges they face in doing business with Jamaican Reggae artists. During the 1980s and 1990s more than twenty Jamaican Reggae acts had international recording contracts with major and large independent record labels in the USA, UK, and Japan. By the beginning of 2015 this number had reduced to fewer than ten. Between 2001 and 2005 Jamaican Reggae/ Dancehall artists Shaggy and Sean Paul released albums that resulted in multi-million copies sold in the USA and globally. In 2014 the top selling current Jamaican Reggae albums were "Fly Rasta" by Ziggy Marley and "Dread and Terrible" by Chronixx, with total album sales between them both of less than 50,000 copies.[3] Almost simultaneously with this decline in Jamaican Reggae business internationally, there has been a noticeable increase in the number of successful North American and European homegrown non-Jamaican Reggae bands. [4] One of the biggest records in North America in 2014 was a Reggae recording by the Canadian band Magic, which recorded sales in excess of 3 million copies in the USA alone [5]

The global music industry has faced major challenges and experienced significant changes and dislocations since the turn of the century, primarily as a consequence of technological innovations and shifts in the entertainment consumption patterns of the public. Like all other music

---

1. http://www.Reggaecontestlatino.com/portal/

2. http://www.Reggaecontest.com/portal/

3. http://www.jamaicaobserver.com/entertainment/Billboard-s-top-15-Reggae-albums-of-2014

4. http://www.npr.org/blogs/therecord/2011/11/17/142254188/non-jamaican-Reggae-whos-making-it-and-whos-buying-it

5. http://www.rollingstone.com/music/features/how-magic-s-canadian-Reggae-took-over-jamaica-20150318

genres, Reggae has also faced these challenges. There are however some peculiar features to the development, creation and promotion of Reggae music that have caused additional roadblocks to business development and the realization of greater economic and social benefits to primary music producers, and the Jamaican economy as a whole.

Accurate data on the economic performance of Reggae inside Jamaica and internationally have been very difficult to come by. This is largely because of the underdeveloped nature of local music trade organizations. This adversely affects their relationships with counterpart international music organizations that play a major role in the collection and dissemination of global music industry revenue information. Music industry performance information provided by the government agency, Statistical Institute of Jamaica is grossly inadequate. Despite the efforts of entities such as the Jamaica Reggae Industry Association/JaRIA, the local industry is still lacking the collective representation required. Valuable lessons could be learned by studying entities such as UK Music. A 2014 UK Music study showed that in 2013 the music industry outperformed the UK economy by growing at 9 percent, compared with the UK economy as a whole, which grew at 1.7 percent.[6] Jamaica's inability to do similar music industry reporting is a significant barrier to development.

The development of Jamaican culture and music must be examined in the context of colonization and slavery. Issues related to the genesis, historical development and promotion of Reggae within Jamaica and internationally, are also inextricably bound with issues related to the development and promotion of Rastafari. There is no question that Bob Marley's rise to fame as an international music superstar is due largely to his Rastaman livity, and the incorporation of Rastafari principles in his music. One can also make the case however, that much of the resistance and lack of support to the development of the business of Reggae stems from cultural, spiritual and political conflicts between principles of Rastafari on the one hand, and what is expected in order to fit and succeed within "the Babylon system".

The business of Reggae music has been the subject of debates for many years, and increasingly so in more recent times.

Among the many issues raised are:
- inadequate and ineffective government support,

---

6. http://www.ukmusic.org/research/measuring-music/

- inadequate training,
- the ignorance of artists,
- ineffective management,
- the lack of appreciation of intellectual property rights,
- failure to adapt and adhere to globally acceptable business practices.

Conflicts, misunderstandings, and misrepresentations regarding issues such as homosexuality, homophobia, criminality, marijuana, and the status of women, have also surfaced from time to time in discussions about Reggae music business development. Some express the view that despite Bob Marley and other successes, the business of Jamaican Reggae has not realized its full potential, at either the local or international levels.

REGGAE ROADBLOCKS explores the many issues that have affected the development of the business of Reggae. Its objective is to generate relevant discussions and facilitate new thinking and approaches to address the various challenges faced by creative, technical and management practitioners of Reggae inside and outside of Jamaica.

REGGAE ROADBLOCKS is not an academic study, but instead represents the author's efforts to share opinions based on his experience in the music industry at both the Jamaican and international levels. Relevant short commentaries written by the author that have been previously published are included throughout the book, and there are web-links to music, music videos and other publications cited. Excerpts from interviews and quotations from well-known Reggae influencers are also included.

To wrap up this introduction, we share the telling perspectives of Copeland Forbes and Chris Blackwell, two individuals who have been deeply involved in the business of Jamaican music for more than 50 years:

Copeland Forbes – Artist Manager and Tour Manager

There are many roadblocks in the business of music that we as Jamaicans create. I think we need to take a more professional approach in what we do. The word business is missing from the heads of a lot of Jamaican artists.

I have been in the business of music since December 1962, coming up through the ranks, from a personal assistant to artist manager and tour manager. I was personal assistant to Peter Tosh. As a personal as-

sistant, I got closer to the artists than even a manager would, and got to know more about how artists think. For example, what people had Peter Tosh to be, is not the man I knew. Peter was the most intelligent person I ever met. That is why he named his company Intel Dilplo. I learned a lot through my experience with Peter Tosh.

The businesslike approach required in Jamaican music has been missing from the early days of international exposure in the 1970s. A lot of artists in those days signed contracts that they did not understand. Artists frequently signed contracts with local music producers who then entered into agreements with international labels and distributors that the artists had no clue about. The provisions for automatic extension of recording and distribution contracts were often misunderstood, leading to artists thinking they were no longer obligated to exclusive recording and distribution deals, when in fact they were. The issue of advances from record companies was also often misunderstood, as artists treated advances as gifts, rather than payments that were recoupable from future royalties. Many artists did not have experienced representation, but instead surrounded themselves with individuals who were interested in profiling. I recall going to a store with an artist manager and recommending that he purchase the book This Business of Music, but instead he bought a camera and an empty briefcase.

The business of music has changed a lot in recent years, and record companies are reluctant to expend large sums on artist advances and tour support. I think a lot of the Jamaican artists today have no long term vision or career plan. They do not work with a team consisting of manager, road manager, publicists, personal assistant, and lawyer. Instead they mostly engage family members and friends who are not qualified.

The support needed from the government is weak. I have been to the Jamaican Government many times with ideas and plans based on what I see on the international scene, but they look at me as if I am speaking a different language. My observation in recent years is that there is growth in European Reggae festivals staged throughout the summer months, with several artists from Jamaica participating. Yet nothing is being done by the Jamaican government to capitalize on these events to generate more revenue inflows to the Jamaican economy.

I have been taking local media representatives with me to some of these international events, so that they will take the news back for broadcast on TV in Jamaica. In 2002 I organized a "One Love USA Tour" in celebration of my 40 years in the music business. There were 57 persons from Jamaica on this tour which was happening at the same time that the theme promoting Jamaican tourism was "One Love", including Jamaican government sponsored advertising on CNN. I called CNN and was told that the cost of a 60-seconds commercial was US$1 Million. I approached two government agencies, Jamaica Promotions Corporation/JAMPRO, and the Jamaica Tourist Board/JTB, as well as local private corporate entities for support for the tour. Absolutely no support was received. I however received support from foreign entities such as American Airlines, Nutrament, and the tour bus company we hired.

In my view Jamaicans are not preparing to be a part of their own thing. We started something good in Reggae, but we have left it alone and have not nurtured it. When you attend a Reggae festival such as Rototom in Spain, a significant portion of the items you see in the booths represent things Jamaican, but are not from Jamaica, nor being sold by Jamaicans.

I have told Jamaican government representatives on several occasions that every major international Reggae festival should have a JAMPRO/JTB sponsored booth under the banner of "Brand Jamaica" with Jamaican made products for sale and promotion.

While the level of Jamaican government support for Reggae is minimal, the artists are also to be blamed for this. Most artists don't want to hear the word taxes, and pay very little attention to accounting and paper work. Not enough attention is placed on the professional aspects of their career.

I often hear government representatives say that they can't fight for support on behalf of the artists, as they do not want to pay taxes. I think the persons in Government that have a responsibility to the music industry are wearing blinkers, and I tell them that. The educational workshops that are presented for music industry practitioners are never attended by those who need the information. Organizers of these workshops do not recognize that they need to entice participants to attend, and that the best way to get strong attendance is to invite relevant international music celebrities to speak.

I ask myself why is it that Jamaican government representatives over the years have failed to recognize the value of Jamaican music and render necessary support, and I have not been able to answer that question. If I were put in a position of responsibility for entertainment in the Jamaican government there would be a big turnaround that would shake people. The very first thing I would focus on is education. There is no point in doing things when the players and stakeholders do not understand. As Peter Tosh would say "You can't change people if you do not change their minds".

In recent years foreign Reggae acts have been doing better business than us, selling more records than us, and getting more attention than us. Why? From my own experience Jamaican Reggae artists priced themselves out of the live show market during the recession. The fees asked by some artists bore no relation whatsoever to demand for their performance, or to record sales.

Some of our major international artists have also acted unscrupulously with international concert promoters, causing a ripple negative effect in turning off event organizers and booking agents in markets such as the USA and Brazil. As a result of these experiences, foreign show promoters and booking agents have shifted their focus away from Jamaican Reggae artists and now pay more attention to non-Jamaican artists such as SOJA, Matisyahu, Rebelution, from the USA, Midnight, from the Virgin Islands, and Gondwana and Los Pericos from South America.

We are making music for ourselves in Jamaica. Sometimes I don't understand what Jamaican artists are singing about. In my view there is not the same emphasis today on the messages in Reggae that resonated worldwide years ago. There is too much music about killing and other negative things. Where is the love that Bob Marley taught us all about?

We are not making music to sell. We are not making music that people can relate to internationally. We are making music for our brethren around the corner, who is also not buying music. I am tired of hearing artists blame international record companies when they get dropped, with the excuse being that the companies don't know how to promote Reggae music. I can tell from personal experience that when you sign to a record company and take with you a professional and experienced team, record deals will work. In many instances record deals are terminated due to the unprofessionalism of the artists. There is no loyalty to commitments made to record companies. Artists sign deals but often do not stay focused to promote and support their own work.

Jamaica is full of talent, but unfortunately some of the new artists are embracing the bad ways of earlier artists. Emerging artists such as Tarrus Riley, Chronixx, Protoje, Kabaka Pyramid, Raging Fyah, Jesse Royal, Jah9, Etana, and others, seem to have their heads in the right place, but if they are not properly guided and open themselves to experienced advice, their efforts could be derailed through negative influences. We do need more artists like these, and we need to work on changing the behavior of other artists who operate in a negative and unprofessional way. It is alleged that most of the artists from Jamaica with unprofessional and negative attitudes in recent years are from the Dancehall genre.

Too many of these Jamaican artists are burdened with immigration problems. To create more positives than negatives we need to educate artists, and artists have to be wise and show a willingness to become more professional."

Chris Blackwell – Island Records/Bob Marley

I believe that the golden age of Jamaican music is definitely behind us, I really do believe that. I say this because of the incredible amount of excellent talent in writing, performing, musicianship, and production that existed in the past that caused a wave that is still traveling around the world. Yes, that same music that was recorded 40-50 years ago created a solid base of music that over the years has continued to evolve.

In order that the local music industry can be further developed there needs to be more clubs, restaurants and cafes where live music can be heard in Jamaica. There are very few at this time because the all-inclusive hotel model does not encourage guests to leave the hotels as all their meals are included in their room rate, thereby killing night life, and in so doing offer no opportunity for visitors to see and hear Jamaican music in Jamaica.

Reggae, Cultural Diversity, and Cultural Heritage

Jamaican culture is manifested by distinct globally recognized features derived from a mixture of influences from African, Caribbean, European and Asian experiences. Reggae music is without doubt the leading global representation of Jamaican culture. This chapter will examine implications for the development of Reggae in the context of the clearly articulated principles of two United Nations conventions on cultural diversity and cultural heritage.

The concept of cultural diversity refers to the cultural variety and cultural differences that exist in the world, or in a particular society. The phrase cultural diversity may also be used in reference to having different cultures respect each other's differences. The many separate nations, societies, and groups that have emerged around the globe differ significantly from each other as a result of the environment within which they have developed. Many of these differences that characterize nations persist today.

The term "Brand Jamaica" is commonly used to describe the cultural traits that uniquely define the island and people of Jamaica. Culture transcends differences in language, dress, religion, and traditions, to include the variety of ways in which communities organize themselves, interact with their environment, and the perceptions of morality held by the members of the community.

Jamaica, like many small countries, has faced tremendous pressure as a result of globalization. Developments in technology in recent decades have caused information and capital to erase geographic boundaries and reshape the relationships between the marketplace, states, and citizens. The growth of the mass media industry has largely impacted individuals and societies across the globe. Although beneficial in many respects, this increased accessibility and flow of information has also demonstrated its capacity to negatively impact a society's individuality, and in some instances even challenge its sovereignty. The emergence of the Internet, and the free flow of media content in and out of Jamaica, have impacted both the culture and music of the Island in positive and negative ways.

There is a school of thought that, with information and creative content being so easily distributed throughout the world, cultural meanings, values and tastes run the risk of becoming homogenized, resulting in the weakening and dilution of the strength of identity of individuals and societies. This is an interesting proposition for examination in the context of Jamaican culture, and in particular Reggae music and Rastafari culture.

The United Nations recognizes the need to protect, promote and preserve cultural heritage and cultural diversity through the implementation of two international conventions:

1. The UNESCO Convention on the Protection and Promotion of the Diversity of Cultural Expression, (2005),[7] and
2. The UNESCO Convention Concerning the Protection of the World Cultural and Natural Heritage, (1972).[8]

The UNESCO Convention on the Protection and Promotion of the Diversity of Cultural Expression has been ratified by Jamaica and close to 120 member states, as well as the European Union. To date the USA and Israel have not ratified the convention. The UNESCO 2005 Convention recognizes the following:

- the distinctive nature of cultural goods, services and activities as vehicles of identity, values and meaning;
- that while cultural goods, services and activities have important economic value, they are not mere commodities or consumer goods that can only be regarded as objects of trade.

---

7. http://www.unesco.org/new/en/culture/themes/cultural-diversity/2005-convention
8. http://whc.unesco.org/en/conventiontext/

The Convention was adopted in response to pressure exerted on countries to waive their right to enforce cultural policies and to put all aspects of the cultural sector on the table when negotiating international trade agreements. It represents a clear recognition of the specific and peculiar nature of cultural goods and services, as well as state sovereignty in the area of culture. The UNESCO 2005 Convention also recognizes that culture can no longer be treated merely as a by-product of development, but rather the mainspring for sustainable development. The Convention ushers in a new international framework for the governance and management of culture by:

- encouraging the introduction of cultural policies and measures that nurture creativity, provide access for creators to participate in domestic and international marketplaces where their artistic works and expressions can be recognized and compensated, and ensure these expressions are accessible to the public at large;
- recognizing and optimizing the overall contribution of the cultural industries to economic and social development, particularly in developing countries;
- integrating culture into sustainable development strategies and national development policies;
- promoting international cooperation to facilitate the mobility of artists as well as the flow of cultural goods and services, especially those from the South.
- Cultural diversity is presented and promoted as the antithesis of cultural uniformity. Many cultural and creative industries experts and practitioners, (including UNESCO), fear the emergence of a trend towards cultural uniformity, partly fueled by globalization. In support of this fear they point to different issues, with examples such as:
- the disappearance of many languages and dialects, or their lack of legal status or protection;
- the anxiety of people in the preservation of their traditions and indigenous practices;
- increasing cultural penetration of foreign countries by the United States through the distribution of its products in film, television, music, clothing and nutrition as promoted by audio-visual media.

The 1972 UNESCO Convention Concerning the Protection of the World Cultural and Natural Heritage has been ratified by Jamaica and over 190 member states. The Convention recognizes that deterioration or disappearance of any item of cultural heritage constitutes a harmful impoverishment of the heritage of all nations of the world. The Convention also clearly states that parts of cultural or natural heritage are of outstanding interest, and therefore need to be preserved as part of the world heritage of mankind as a whole.

Rastafari is as a belief system rooted in African ancestry while simultaneously establishing a unique society reflected in the artistic documentation of Jamaican history. It is the view of many that the Government and people of Jamaica have not done enough to adhere to the aims and objectives of the UNESCO World Heritage Convention in their treatment of Rastafari culture.

The debate surrounding the call for protection and preservation of Pinnacle, the first Rastafari community in Jamaica, provides an interesting study regarding the implementation of this Convention. The Pinnacle debacle in Jamaica placed the Rastafari community in direct confrontation with government and big private investors about the pursuit of a strict commercial agenda, versus cultural   heritage preservation. This resulted in the establishment by Bob Marley's grand-daughter Donisha Prendergast, of the "Occupy Pinnacle" movement. [9]

Cultural Diversity in Jamaica and the Development of Reggae

Jamaica has a very strong and vibrant culture. On the surface it may seem to be homogenous, but Jamaican culture is actually very diverse. It represents a combination of cultures that have inhabited the Island. The original Taino settlers were followed by their Spanish conquerors, who were in turn conquered by the British, and they all made contributions to the development of Jamaican culture. It is however the Black slaves from Africa who became the dominant cultural influence, as they suffered and resisted the harsh conditions of forced labour. After the abolition of slavery, Chinese and Indian migrants were transported to the Island as workers, bringing with them ideas

---

9. https://www.facebook.com/groups/occupypinnacle/

from the Far East. Jamaica's motto "Out of Many, One People" exemplifies the diverse nature of the Jamaican population.

The official language in Jamaica is English, but a local dialect called Patois (Patwa) is spoken by a very large percentage of the population. Jamaican Patois originated from a combination of English, Spanish and African phrases with more rhythmic sounds than traditional English. Patois is spoken and understood by Jamaicans of all ethnic origins, and is the primary means of communication in the lyrics of Jamaican music.

Christianity is by far the largest religion in Jamaica, with the Roman Catholic, Anglican, and Church of God denominations figuring most prominently. A popular anecdotal saying is that Jamaica has the most churches per square mile of any country in the world. Rastafari is a derivative of the larger Christian culture, but its origins are deeply influenced by consciousness about Africa and an awareness of current political and historical events on that continent. Rastafari is a belief system based on teachings found in the Bible, particularly the Book of Revelation, as well as the philosophies and teachings of Haile Selassie I, Marcus Garvey and Leonard Howell, the founder of Pinnacle. Rastafari distinguishes itself from Christianity in that Rastas believe in the divinity of Emperor Haile Selassie. Strong Christian religious traditions, and the resistance movement of Rastafari, have had the greatest impact on the shaping of Jamaican music. Many well-known Jamaican singers either started out singing in church choirs, or are influenced by Rastafari.

The lyrical themes and rhythms that have come to define Reggae music are derived predominantly from African cultural influences. The integration of cultures from former European colonial powers Spain and England, and the Chinese and Indian indentured workers from the Far East have also played a role in influencing the development of Jamaican music. The unique sounds that have been presented to the world as Mento, Ska, Rocksteady, Reggae, and now Dancehall, result from the interplay and diverse influences in the cultural melting pot that is Jamaica. Jamaica's ethnic and racial diversity has also been represented and reflected by internationally successful artists such as Bob Marley, Super Cat, Byron Lee, Sean Paul, and Tessanne Chin.

Although slavery was abolished in the 19th century, colonialism continued, and living conditions for the majority of Jamaicans were not improved. Exploitation and domination by former slave masters merely took on a different dimension. The Rastafari movement and Reggae music emerged as leading vehicles through which people expressed discontent, and their demands for self-recognition, socio-economic upliftment, and political determination. By the 1970s Reggae was recognized as an avenue to transmit ideas, define and affirm values, and express expectations. It did not confine itself to Jamaica, but was exported throughout the Caribbean and the Jamaican diaspora, particularly into England as a result of the migration of thousands of Jamaicans.

The character, definition and global appreciation for Reggae music were shaped by the works of Jamaica-based artists such as Bob Marley, Peter Tosh, Toots and the Maytals, Jimmy Cliff, Desmond Dekker, Dennis Brown, Third World, Black Uhuru, Burning Spear, Freddie McGregor, Culture, Marcia Griffiths, Bob Andy, Gregory Isaacs and others. Significant contribution was also made by overseas based artists such as Linton Kwesi Johnson, Steel Pulse, Aswad, Lucky Dube, Maxi Priest, UB 40, and Alpha Blondy. Many initial Reggae recordings reflected the atmosphere of the Jamaican slums which nurtured them. Lyrical themes also spoke to issues of captivity and the Rastaman's desire to return to Africa. The struggles of black heroes were also documented in song, with many references to Marcus Garvey and Nelson Mandela for example. The peculiar Afro Caribbean cultural experience of Jamaicans living in Kingston slums, and their influence on artists in other countries determined the international face of what has been described as roots Reggae.

In more recent years the view has been expressed that the development of Jamaican music has suffered somewhat from the impact of cultural penetration from the United States. While traditional roots Reggae remains popular outside Jamaica, the Dancehall sub-genre has become more popular in recent years among young Jamaicans. Most Dancehall is heavily influenced by American Hip-Hop lifestyle and themes, and several Jamaican Dancehall songs are being created on pseudo-Hip Hop beats. Unlike traditional roots Reggae, much of Dancehall music appeals to materialistic and sexual instincts, and glorify violence and the use of guns.

Katrina Lacey, of Arizona State University, in her article "Rastafari, Reggae, and Resistance" in the spring 2005 issue of *e-misférica*, the journal of the Hemispheric Institute of Performance and Politics, argues that while Reggae and Rasta culture continue as viable forms of protest and resistance, the trend to materialistic lyrics is brought on by the culture's acceptance into the mainstream, including recognition by the Grammys, and this has pushed the music "away from the realm of revolutionary practice and closer to the realm of performance as product and commodity."[10]

The UNESCO 2005 Convention on the Protection and Promotion of the Diversity of Cultural Expression speaks directly to the issue of cultural penetration by countries such as the USA. While Jamaica has ratified the Convention, enough has not been done at the local level to further the implementation of the principles of the Convention. This is to a great degree attributable to relative inactivity on the part of successive Jamaican government administrations. Does this amount to a Reggae Roadblock?

Reggae, Technology and Music Production

Music production and promotion in Jamaica have been at the cutting edge with regard to innovation and the use of technology since the 1960s. Innovative technological experiments were employed by studio recording engineers, music producers, electronics technicians and promoters in the creation of Dub music and the Jamaican sound systems. The manipulation of recorded music tracks for re-mixing, and the experimentation with recording studio effects such as echo, reverb, and panoramic delay by Jamaican recording engineers and music producers date back more than 50 years. Jamaicans can therefore stake claim to be pioneers of this type of recording technology which has expanded to become globally practiced in a variety of music genres.

The first Jamaican sound systems were designed and built with large custom made speaker cabinets and powerful amplifiers with technologically advanced capacity to distinguish and enhance treble, mid-range and bass frequencies. Jamaican musician and electronics genius Hedley Jones is credited as the person who defined the bourgeoning Jamaican sound system technology. The equipment used by the leading sound system op-

---

10. https://hemi.nyu.edu/journal/2_1/lacey.html

erators and music producers in the 1960s and 1970s (Clement "Coxsone" Dodd of Studio 1, and Arthur "Duke" Reid) were built by Jones.

The emergence and evolution of dub music and Jamaican sound system technologies would possibly not have occurred without the creative and innovative genius of Osbourne "King Tubby" Ruddock. King Tubby is known primarily for his influence on the development of dub music and Jamaican sound systems in the late 1950s through the 60s and 70s. His innovative work in music studios elevated the role of the mixing engineer to a creative position that was formerly attributable only to musicians, vocalists and composers. His techniques of modifying original music and vocal tracks and introducing effects such as delays, echoes, reverb and phase effects, resulted in the creation of new, sometimes unrecognizable, versions of prior existing sound recordings. These techniques have been expanded to influence a wide range of new and traditional popular music genres. Tubby can stake claim to being the inventor of the concept of re-mixing upon which genres such as Dance and Electronic music are built. His studio innovations and music production work in the 1970s made him one of the best known music celebrities of the time inside Jamaica, and also generated interest in his work from music producers, sound engineers and musicians around the world.

The late 1980s and early 1990s also heralded another period of technological innovation in Jamaican music that has had very significant impact on popular music production globally. In 1986 keyboardist Wycliffe "Steely" Johnson and drummer Cleveland "Clevie" Browne became the resident session musicians for Lloyd "King Jammy" James, a protege of King Tubby. Steely & Clevie, as they became popularly known, were responsible for the introduction and popularizing in Jamaica of the use of drum machines and synthesizers for the recording of music tracks. Their innovations in music production led to the explosion of digital recording, and the rise of what has become popularly known as Dancehall rhythms and Dancehall music.

The digital multimedia and Internet revolution being experienced globally has significantly impacted the business of Reggae in Jamaica, particularly with regard to the use of social media. It is fair to say that increased reliance on social media as a promotional tool by the younger generation of Jamaican recording artists and music producers has lessened the negative impact of Payola. Payola, (the unofficial system of pay for play in traditional media, which is illegal in the USA), has been a major challenge for artists in Jamaica. The embrace of social media for promotion has also contributed to the resurgence in popularity of roots Reggae music inside Jamaica. This resurgence, or Reggae Revival, has been fueled by the synergies and linkages between the visual and performing arts, making content more attractive for social media exposure. Reggae Revival artists who have effectively combined and used music, visual arts and social media include Chronixx[11] and Protoje.[12]

Marketing Reggae in a Culturally Diverse World

Today the market for Reggae music transcends geographic, cultural and ethnic boundaries. The mass migration of Jamaicans to England that began in the 1950s has resulted in the development of large immigrant communities of Reggae and Rastafari supporters. Reggae/Rasta influences in the UK have also been exported to countries on the European continent. Rastafari's growth and penetration in Africa and the America's has also contributed to the development of communities of Reggae music supporters in many countries.

Countries with significant numbers of Reggae music fans now include, the USA and Canada in North America; the UK, Germany, France, Spain, Netherlands, Italy, and Sweden in Europe; Brazil, Colombia, Argentina, Chile, Panama, Costa Rica, Puerto Rico in Latin America; Kenya, Ghana, South Africa, Ivory Coast, Senegal, Uganda, Zimbabwe, and Tanzania in Africa, as well as Japan, Australia and New Zealand. In addition to the creation of international Reggae music fans, this global phenomenon has resulted in the birth of many home-grown non-Jamaican Reggae artists who record and perform in a variety of languages, mainly French, Spanish, Japanese, Portuguese, German, and Swahili.

In examining the marketing of Reggae from Jamaica to the culturally diverse world market, a key consideration should be the fact that Jamaican music is typically recorded and performed in English or Jamaican Patois. While many non-English speaking Reggae fans still do appreciate and relate to Jamaican made Reggae, there is no doubt that market penetration limitations exist due to language barriers.

Many Jamaica-based Reggae recording artists (particularly the

---

11. https://www.facebook.com/chronixxmusic
12. https://www.facebook.com/protoje

younger performers in the Dancehall sub-genre), also tend to write songs addressing issues and themes of a local parochial nature. This brand of Reggae is often not understood outside of the ethnic Jamaican or Caribbean communities, and therefore has limited international market potential. The incorporation of more standard English and foreign languages, with production and performance collaborations between Jamaica-based artists and their non-English speaking colleagues would likely result in greater levels of global market penetration. Similarly, the recording and performance of songs with lyrics addressing issues and themes that can relate to a wider non-Jamaican international audience, will contribute to greater levels of global market penetration.

The international marketing of Reggae made by artists from non-Jamaican communities requires consideration of the specificities of these communities, including the limitations experienced by these artists. Many non-Jamaican Reggae artists record songs in their mother language and experience challenges in gaining acceptance outside of their domestic markets. For example some popular Reggae artists from Japan and Germany have been known to experience major success at home, yet at the same time having little or no presence in other countries. Creative collaborations with Jamaica-based artists are often used as a means of addressing this challenge. Home-grown Reggae artists in larger music markets such as the USA, Germany, the UK, Japan, France, Canada, and Brazil do however have the marketing advantage of being better able to tour and promote their music in their homeland. Jamaica-based Reggae artists are on the other hand hampered by the often stringent work visa requirements that prevent effective marketing and promotion in some of these larger markets. An example of successful collaborations between foreign artists and Jamaicans include SOJA from the USA with Damian Marley:[13]

Global marketing challenges and opportunities have resulted in what was defined by Jamaican television producer Winford Williams as "The Changing Face of Reggae". In his local TV series "On Stage" Williams looks at a number of issues, including the rise in popularity of white Reggae bands based in the USA and their dominance of the live music circuit and American national Reggae sales charts. Recorded Reggae music

---

13. https://www.youtube.com/watch?v=rd_nITGyRSo

by American bands such as SOJA, The Green, Matisyahu, Groundation, Rebelution currently outsell music by their Jamaican counterparts.[14]

Developments within the international Reggae music festival circuit also provide an interesting study in the global marketing of Reggae. In recent years support has grown in Jamaica and internationally for the annual Rebel Salute festival that emphasizes traditional roots Reggae. Despite this, Jamaica-based music festivals have mostly struggled to remain viable due to inadequate and inconsistent funding and other support. The Reggae festival markets in Europe and the West Coast of the USA appear to be more buoyant, and have increased in numbers.

Jamaica's premier summer Reggae festival "Reggae Sumfest" continues to resort to the inclusion of American R&B and Hip-Hop artists as main attractions, while European and California Reggae festivals attract large crowds with almost 100 percent Reggae line-ups. The competition from the summer European Reggae festival circuit for the services of the top Jamaican artists is so strong that Jamaica's Sumfest promoters have publicly declared that they are being forced to examine the possibility of a change in the timing of the presentation of their event. [15] Inside the USA the Cali Roots Festival has experienced growth and now has a brand that is spreading outside that state.[16]

Reggae music has expanded widely around the world, more so than any other music form originating from a small developing country. Marketing Reggae music in this very culturally diverse global space therefore requires a level of sophistication that to date has not been acknowledged or applied from within Jamaica. Jamaica continues to operate without a clearly defined national cultural industry policy that provides for structured development of its music industry, including marketing strategies at both the domestic and international levels.

Jamaican Homophobia and Reggae

As is the case in many other countries, members of the Jamaican lesbian, gay, bisexual and transgender (LGBT) community face legal and social issues not experienced by non-LGBT people. In Jamaica however,

---

14. http://vimeo.com/68907156

15. http://jamaica-gleaner.com/gleaner/20140805/ent/ent1.html.

16. http://www.kionrightnow.com/news/local-news/monterey-Reggae-festival-brings-in-12-million-for-local-economy/27596604

sexual acts between men are punishable under the law with up to ten years imprisonment. The Jamaican law does not criminalize the status of being LGBT, but instead outlaws the conduct. Section 76 of the Jamaica Offences Against the Person Act provides as follows:

"Whosoever shall be convicted of the abominable crime of buggery... shall be liable to be imprisoned and kept to hard labour for a term not exceeding ten years."

Sexual acts between women are not addressed by the Jamaican law, and are therefore by omission legal. There is no law in Jamaica that prevents discrimination on the basis of sexual orientation, gender identity or gender expression. Many Jamaicans oppose the inclusion of sexual orientation as a human right. It is argued that to do so would be alien to Jamaican culture, with its strong traditional Christian religious beliefs.

Jamaica has been described by some human rights groups as one of the most homophobic countries in the world. According to a 2012 report by the Inter-American Commission on Human Rights, "discrimination based on sexual orientation, gender identity, and gender expression is widespread throughout Jamaica." The government of Jamaica however declared in the same year that it is committed to the equal and fair treatment of its citizens, and affirms that any individual whose rights are alleged to have been infringed, has a right to seek redress. The government also claimed that there is no legal discrimination against persons on the grounds of their sexual orientation, and that it is opposed to discrimination or violence against persons whatever their sexual orientation.

Many Jamaicans claim that Jamaica's reputation as one of the most homophobic countries in the world is unjustified, and that it is merely propaganda, and point to the fact that life in Jamaica for LGBT persons was improving.

The vast majority of Jamaicans have a negative view of homosexuality. This is borne out in the "National Survey of Attitudes and Perceptions of Jamaicans Towards Same Sex Relations" published in 2011. According to this survey, 85.2 percent of Jamaicans aged 18 to 84 were opposed to legalizing homosexuality among consenting adults. 82.2 percent said that male homosexuality was immoral, and 75.2 percent believed that female homosexuality was immoral. Most Jamaicans attribute their anti-gay stance to their strong Christian beliefs, and base their position on religious grounds.

Strong anti-gay sentiments also exist within the Rastafari movement. Rastas regard sex between men as unhygienic. A few Rastas have however spoken out in favour of gay rights, and consider the persecution of people because of sexual orientation to be contradictory to Rastafari traditions as freedom fighters and liberators.

The recording and performance of music is a very significant element of Jamaican popular culture. Musicians in Jamaica are very influential, and also represent and reflect to a great extent popular opinion. A number of prominent Jamaican Dancehall and Reggae artists have been severely criticized and labelled as promoting homophobia and violence against gays due to the lyrics of their songs. Included among these are: Buju Banton, Bounty Killer, Beenie Man, Mavado, Sizzla, Elephant Man, Capleton, T.O.K., and Shabba Ranks.

The international gay rights community, led by the British LGB organization "Outrage" have come out in defense of gay rights, and have launched an ongoing campaign that has adversely affected the careers of many of these artists, and as some would argue, also done severe damage to the global image of Jamaican Reggae and Dancehall music. In defense of the artists and the Reggae and Dancehall music genres, it is said that the music they perform is merely a reflection of Christian and Rastafarian values. The activities of "Outrage" have been labelled by the Black Music Council, a British organisation formed in 2004, as "extremist and racist" for being allegedly intolerant toward Afro-Caribbean culture and music.

Despite a reported decline in the membership of "Outrage", the organization remains active, and has spearheaded the launch in the UK and Canada of what is called the "Stop Murder Music" campaign. The campaign was designed to oppose the alleged homophobic works of some Jamaican artists, primarily of the Dancehall music genre. The "Stop Murder Music" campaign also led to the development of an agreement in 2007 known as "The Reggae Compassionate Act",[17] which some artists agreed to sign. The "Reggae Compassionate Act" has however been somewhat discredited, as most artists refused to sign, and some have denied signing it.

The impact of the "Stop Murder Music" campaign on the global Reggae music community has been severe, from an economic standpoint. There was very little organized representation to protect the over-all good

17. http://www.soulrebels.org/dancehall/w_compassionate_001.htm

international image and reputation of Reggae music. Numerous live concert performances around the world, particularly in the UK, Europe, Canada, and the United States, have been cancelled as a result of demonstrations and protests from the gay rights community. Within the context of the UNESCO 2005 Convention, is there room for a legitimate debate to be had regarding the promotion and protection of Jamaica's religious and cultural practices and beliefs about homosexuality?

Marijuana Culture and Reggae

When the average person thinks Reggae, they almost always make an association with Rastafari and marijuana. Reggae music's most well-known exponent Bob Marley, through the messages in his music and his lifestyle, has possibly contributed the most to this association. The inclusion of lyrical themes in Reggae that advocate resistance to the status quo, peace and love among peoples of all races, and the opening of the mind to higher insights and reasoning through the use of marijuana, have all been very appealing to youths around the world. The perceived direct association of Reggae with Rastafari and marijuana has resulted in misleading stereotyping, as Reggae music is not always about Rastafari, and not all Reggae artists smoke marijuana.

The development of the Rastafari movement in Jamaica does incorporate the spiritual use of marijuana, and the rejection of the degenerate society of materialism and oppression. Members of the Rastafari movement use marijuana in worship as a sacrament, and as an aid to meditation. It is seen as the "Tree of Life" mentioned in the Bible, and many musicians, including Peter Tosh, have quoted Revelation: 22:2. *"...and the leaves of the tree were for the healing of the nations..."* also in reference to its medicinal qualities. It is often smoked in pipes called chalices in sessions where members come together to reason and discuss life issues according to the Rasta perspective. Although the smoking of marijuana is not absolutely necessary for one to be a Rasta, most do use it regularly as a part of their faith, and see the use of the herb as bringing one closer to Jah, allowing one to see the truth of things more clearly.

Rastafari doctrine and the use of marijuana have become significant elements in the making, presentation and promotion of Reggae music. A visit to most music recording studios in Jamaica will almost certainly expose one to musicians, music producers, and recording artists partaking in the smoking of marijuana. Marijuana use at Reggae music festivals has also become an accepted part of the musical celebration. In some places it is not uncommon to see persons openly selling marijuana to concert patrons. The connection between Marijuana and Reggae has been highlighted in numerous recordings by Jamaican artists over the past several decades, ranging from Marley and Tosh, to today's new and rising Reggae stars such as Protoje, Jesse Royal, and Jah9.

While the association of the "herb" with Reggae can be explained through Rastafari beliefs regarding its sacramental, inspirational, and medicinal value, there is also evidence that many young people have been attracted to Reggae merely by virtue of their desire to partake in smoking for recreational purposes.

Despite the widespread use and the promotion of marijuana by many Reggae artists, prohibition of possession remains the focus of the laws of Jamaica and most countries around the world. The legality of marijuana varies from country to country, but possession has been illegal in most countries since prohibition laws started coming into force in the 1920s and 30s. Several countries, particularly in South America, and Europe, and some States in the USA, have decriminalized the possession of small amounts of marijuana. Possession is effectively legal in the Netherlands and Uruguay, and in the states of Colorado and Washington. In December 2013, Uruguay became the first country to legalize the sale, cultivation and distribution of Cannabis. Within the United States there has been a significant shift towards making medical marijuana legal. As of June 2014, twenty three states in the USA had legalized marijuana for medical use. By the end of 2014 there were four states in the USA that had also legalized recreational use of marijuana. These are Alaska, Oregon, Colorado and Washington.

With this trend towards decriminalization and legalization, the government of Jamaica has come under severe pressure from the Rastafari and Reggae community locally and internationally for its apparent tardiness in dealing with marijuana law reform. In April 2015 amendments to the Jamaican Dangerous Drugs Act came into effect, and possession of small quantities of Marijuana in Jamaica is no longer a criminal offense, but one may still be subject to a ticket and a fine. Jamaican Reggae artists continue to lobby and campaign for the full legalization of the herb[18], and mainstream music industry publications such as Billboard Magazine have carried relevant articles on the issue. [19]

Due to the illegality associated with marijuana possession in Jamaica, the use and promotion of marijuana by Reggae artists, in particular those identified with Rastafari, has over the years resulted in arrests, convictions, and the revocation of travel visas. Jamaica also has a well-documented history of police brutality against Reggae artists who use marijuana. The destruction in 1954 by police of the Rastafari community at Pinnacle, is regarded by many in the Rastafari and Reggae music communities as a landmark incident that epitomized the ongoing persecution of Rastafari by the Jamaican Government. Police action against Reggae artists for marijuana use, has resulted in tension between many artists and the government. Resistance by artists to Jamaican government involvement in the local music industry has been one of the side-effects of this strained relationship.

Reggae music has earned its unique place in the world of popular culture as a result of a mixture of influences. The impact of Rastafari and marijuana is very significant. So too are the effects of Christianity and the style of government imposed by Jamaica's colonial and post-colonial leaders. Music feeds from historical and cultural experiences, while simultaneously impacting the lives of persons with diverse cultural backgrounds. Jamaica's role in the future of the business of Reggae internationally, will of necessity require appropriate recognition and treatment of findings from an in-depth analysis of the history of the development of the music and its global impact.

Through REGGAE ROADBLOCKS it is hoped that we can make a contribution to advancing the discussion at the appropriate level, with a view to finding and implementing real solutions.

Summary

- Jamaican culture is reflected in distinct globally recognized features and Reggae music is the leading representation of Jamaican culture.
- Religion and the retention of African customs (Christianity and Ras-

---

18. http://www.jamaicaobserver.com/entertainment/Artistes-add-voice-to-legalisation-push_18844170

19. http://www.billboard.com/biz/articles/news/legal-and-management/6429593/legalize-it-marijuanas-relationship-with-Reggae-and:

tafari), have played a significant role in shaping cultural and moral values in Jamaica and this is reflected in Reggae music.

- The UN convention on protection of cultural diversity raises questions regarding the treatment of homosexuality and homophobia in Jamaican culture, notably Reggae music.
- Global cultural diversity significantly impacts marketing strategies for Reggae.
- Jamaica's diverse cultural experience that embraces African, British, Spanish and North American influences contributes to wide global appeal.
- The use and promotion of marijuana in Reggae music is a cultural practice that has resulted in discrimination and police brutality against artists.
- New global trends and thinking in favour of marijuana decriminalization and legalization offers significant economic opportunities for Jamaica.

Rastafari and Reggae

Music has always played an important role in Rastafari, and Rastafari an important role in Reggae music. The connection between Rasta and Reggae has become well known globally, attributable mainly to the life and work of Bob Marley, along with other artists such as Peter Tosh, Bunny Wailer, Culture, and Burning Spear.

The Origins of Rastafari

Several books and reports have documented Rastafari as emerging in Jamaica in the early 1930s. One of the pioneering reports, "The Rastafari Movement in Kingston, Jamaica"–(July 20, 1960), was presented after a study conducted by the then University College of the West Indies – now University of the West Indies (UWI) – at the request of some prominent members of the movement. Its aim was to examine and prepare an account of the genesis, growth, doctrines, organization, aspirations, needs and conditions of Rastafari in Jamaica for presentation to the government and the then Premier of Jamaica, Norman Washington Manley. Three noted members of staff of the UCWI, Roy Augier, Rex Nettleford and M.G. Smith were commissioned to meet and conduct interviews with brethren from the movement and to compile this report.

According to the report, by the 1920s Marcus Mosiah Garvey had attained the status of prophet and inspirational leader in the minds of many Jamaicans. He had founded the Universal Negro Improvement Association (UNIA) in the United States, proclaimed black nationalism, and preached "Africa for the Africans at home and abroad – One God one aim one destiny." Garvey sought to unite Africans around the world with a central focus on building a united African state. His efforts included the formation of a trading corporation in the United States and the establishment of a shipping line "The Black Star Line" to provide the necessary connection between Africans in the West and the motherland. His impact was truly global, with representation and followers of the UNIA from Jamaica, Costa Rica, Panama, England, and throughout the United States, as well as into several African countries.

Garvey's teachings are said by many Rastas to have included his recommendation to his people to look to Africa for the crowning of a black king, for the day of deliverance would be near. On November 2nd 1930, Tafari Makonnen was crowned in Ethiopia as His Imperial Majesty Haile Selassie I, Conquering Lion of the Tribe of Judah, King of Kings and Elect of God. The Daily Gleaner in Jamaica featured his coronation on the front page of an issue in November 1930. Some Jamaican followers of Garvey, were inspired by the coronation of Ras Tafari, and with the aid of a number of supporting biblical references came to the understanding and acceptance of the doctrine that Ras Tafari was the Living God.

Leonard Percival Howell is referenced as the first person to preach the divinity of Ras Tafari. He started his preaching in Kingston and then moved to St. Thomas, eventually settling with the establishment of a large community of followers at Pinnacle in the hills of St. Catherine parish from 1940 to 1954. Pinnacle became a successful self-sufficient Rastafari community that included the farming of marijuana and other agricultural produce. While Leonard Howell was the most influential and well known preacher and teacher of the doctrines of Rastafari, there were other groups developing simultaneously in Jamaica that pursued a more secular stream.

Some of these include groups from the West Kingston "Dungle", or Back a Wall, in the area now known as Tivoli Gardens, led by Paul Earlington, Vernal Davis and Ferdinand Ricketts. They were more focused on discussing Garvey's teachings about African unity, African self-reliance, and political and economic independence, and the social conditions in Jamaica which justified these teachings. Their emphasis was more on social reform in Jamaica as well as migration to Africa. Other foundational proponents of the Rastafari doctrine include H. Archibald Dunkley.

In Jamaica Rastafari has had a history of many run-ins and altercations with state authorities and the police. Leonard Howell is reported to have been arrested somewhere in the region of fifty times. In 1941 police took action against occupants of Pinnacle, hundreds were arrested, including Howell, who was tried, convicted and sentenced to two years in prison in Spanish Town. In 1954 Pinnacle was dismantled by police, and in 1960 Howell was confined to a mental hospital. The Rastafari uprising that took place in Coral Gardens, Montego Bay, in April 1963, is an indelible monument for Rastafari. A skirmish between Rastafarians and the police resulted in the killing of eight persons. Many reports allege that innocent Rastafarians were murdered.[20]

Over the years many criminals have falsely professed Rasta, and adopted the physical appearance of Rasta – beard and locks. There is a perceived connection between Rastas and criminals, which is emphasized through the association of Rastas with hardened criminals from interaction during and after sentences in prison, often on ganja charges. The criminal element associated with Rasta has existed to the detriment of the more orderly and peaceful representation of Rastafari. The vast majority of Rastafarians have remained peaceful law abiding members of society, although they continue to show defiance to the establishment, through sacramental use of marijuana, while also strongly advocating African unity, economic and political independence for Africans, and the establishment of a united Africa.

Rastafari Doctrine and Organization

The main sources of Rastafari doctrine are from the Old Testament books of the Bible that is the source of many of the dietary observances, some justification of wearing dreadlocks, gender relations and the origin of the name JAH in the Psalms. It is also the source of the Davidic roots of the Ethiopian monarchy, as well as the titles in the book of Revelation that accord with the titles of H.I.M. Those tenets cut across all the groups or mansions of Rastafari I will discuss later. In addition the 12 Tribes of Israel take the blessing of his children by Jacob and the selection of 12

---

20. http://jamaica-gleaner.com/gleaner/20030417/cornwall/cornwall4.html

decuples by Jesus Christ as a justification for the source of the organization's name and designation of members into tribes.

Garvey's influence has already been identified as the main catalyst for the ideas or African unity, redemption and repatriation. Another important Africa-related influence is connected with the Nyabinghi anticolonial cult of east central Africa.

As the worldwide Ethiopianism movement, including the nascent Rastafari, mobilized support against Italy's increasing aggression toward Ethiopia, fascist propaganda reported that Haile Selassie had been elected by Africans at a congress in the USSR to head a secret society known as Nya Binghi, whose aim was the killing of whites. The *Jamaica Times* newspaper of the day carried an English translation of a two part article that appeared in the Vienna, Austria *Neues Wiener Tagblatt*, August 17 (p7)[21] and 24 (p9)[22] 1935, that claimed "millions of blacks from all African nations have formed a secret society [headed by Haile Selassie] for the annihilation of the white race".

Much as Rastafari had emerged in the West in response to slavery's fallout, colonialism and cultural domination by Europeans, Nyabinghi is reported to have arisen in east central Africa (Rwanda, Uganda) as a woman-dominated revivalist sect resisting the late 19th and early 20th century European (British, German and Belgian) incursion and division of Africa. (Peterson, Derek R. "Religious Movements in Southern Uganda". Ethnic Patriotism and the East African Revival: A History of Dissent. Cambridge University Press, 2012. p50.) These were said by anthropologists to have been preceded by a possession cult with the same name. In Jamaica, Rasta began to use the name Nyah-man and Nyabinghi evolved as a group within the movement, the descriptor of a ceremony and of the chants and drumming at such gatherings

Rastafari is made up of a diverse group of individuals who are connected in lifestyle and philosophy, while at the same time enabling individuality in self-development. There are conflicting viewpoints as to whether Rastafari is a religion. The majority view however is that Rastafari is a belief system, and not a religion. There are two very clear common features of Rastafari:

---

21. http://anno.onb.ac.at/cgi-content/anno?aid=nwt&datum=19350817&seite=7&zoom=33
22. http://anno.onb.ac.at/cgi-content/anno?aid=nwt&datum=19350824&seite=9&zoom=33

- The significance placed on Haile Selassie I as a symbol of unity and inspiration, ranging from accepting His Imperial Majesty (H.I.M.) as the "Living God", to revering H.I.M. as the single most important motivational force and inspiration for Rastafari.
- That salvation can come to black people only through repatriation to Africa.

With the exception of the two above mentioned common features, the opinions and lifestyle practices of Rastafarians vary widely. For example some Rastas wear beards and some don't. Not all Rastafarians wear locks. Some Rastafarians smoke marijuana, but many don't. Many Rastafarians maintain high moral principles, while at the other extreme some are alleged to be involved in crime and violence. Some Rastas are excellent workmen and artisans, while others avoid work. The health and nutritional practices of Rastas also vary. Rastafari doctrine consistently rejects the consumption of pork, and many Rastafarians adhere to a strict vegetarian diet, while others eat fish and other meats.

The Rastafari community can be characterized as being disorganized and resistant to structures. It also suffers from significant leadership weaknesses. The majority of Rastas are not attached to any of the organizations or Rastafari Mansions that exist. There also appears to be no leader or group of leaders who can speak for the movement as a whole, or define its doctrines.

Rastafari Mansions

The "Mansions" of Rastafari are the recognized branches of the Rastafari community. The term is derived from the Biblical verse "In my father's house are many mansions," – John 14:2. The main mansions of Rastafari are: the Nyabinghi, the Bobo Shanti, and the Twelve Tribes of Israel.

Nyabinghi – The Nyabinghi order is the oldest of the Rastafari mansions. Members of the Nyabinghi order are known to be strongly against war and violence and are advocates of anti-racism. Nyabinghi resistance has been a major inspiration to many Jamaican Rastafarians who have incorporated Nyabinghi practices such as chanting and burning the likeness of oppressors in fire, into their celebrations. These chants are accompanied by drumming. Three types of drums are used in Nyabinghi:

bass, funde and akete. Notable Nyabinghi Reggae artists include Ras Michael and Count Ossie.

Bobo Shanti – The Bobo Shanti order was founded in 1958 in Jamaica by Prince Emanuel Charles Edwards. The Bobo Shanti advocate for the return of all black people to Africa, and for reparations in the form of monetary compensation and reimbursement to black people for slavery. Prince Emanuel is regarded as part of a holy trinity in which Haile Selassie 1 is Jah, Marcus Garvey is prophet, and Emanuel is high priest. The Bobo Shanti live apart from society and other Rastafari orders and are primarily based in the Nine Miles area of Bull Bay, in Jamaica. They are a self-sufficient group who do their own farming, and they also dress differently, wearing tightly wrapped turbans and long robes. Some notable Bobo Shanti Reggae artists include The Abyssinians, Junior Reid, Capleton, Anthony B, Sizzla Kalonji, Junior Kelly, JahMason, Lutan Fyah, Fantan Mojah and Pressure.

Twelve Tribes of Israel – The Twelve Tribes of Israel is a Rastafarian group founded in 1968 in Trench Town, Jamaica by Vernon Carrington, also known as Prophet Gad. He started the organization under the umbrella of Charter 15 of the Ethiopian World Federation. The membership of the Twelve Tribes has spread worldwide with functioning branches in several countries. The Twelve Tribes accept Jesus Christ as Master and Saviour. They see Haile Selassie I as a king in the lineage of David and Solomon, who is divinely chosen by the creator to represent him on earth. A 12 tribes greeting at its meetings describes Haile Selassie as Christ in his kingly character. The Twelve Tribes practice the use of symbols based on the twelve sons of Jacob that correspond with the months of the ancient Israelite calendar beginning with April and Reuben. Bob Marley is identified as coming from the tribe of Joseph by virtue of his birthdate in February. So is Dennis Brown. Other prominent Rastafarian Reggae artist members of the Twelve Tribes of Israel include Freddie McGregor. Like the Nyabinghi order, the Twelve Tribes of Israel are anti-racist.

Other "Mansions of Ras Tafari" include the Haile Selassie I School of Vision, the Royal Ethiopian Judah Coptic Church, the Ethiopian Zion Coptic Church, the International Peace Makers, the Leonard P. Howell Foundation, the Haile Selassie I Theocracy Government, the Dreaded Nyahbinghi, Camp David, and the Rastafari Centralization Organization. In addition there is the Ethiopian Orthodox Church and the Ethiopian

World Federation, which are not strictly speaking Rastafarian organizations, but their membership in Jamaica com-prises mainly Rasta.

In 2007 the Ethio-Africa Diaspora Millennium Council or Rastafari Millennium Council (RMC), was formed with headquarters in Kingston, Jamaica. The RMC was established with representation on its governing council from several Mansions of Rastafari, with a mission to unify the community and provide collective representation. In recent years there has been much controversy regarding the leadership and legitimacy of the governing council of the RMC, and there has also not been much unification within the community. Despite the growth of Rastafari, the expansion of the community to include several mansions, and efforts to establish the RMC, there is still evidence of discrimination and marginalization, and collective representation is weak. Members of the Rastafari community also attribute many of the roadblocks and challenges faced in the development of the Reggae industry to discrimination and marginalization of Rastafari.

In research work conducted by South African indigenous rights lawyer Roger Chennels in 2007, the structure and development of the Rastafari movement was analyzed and the following needs and challenges revealed:

- the need to strengthen the RMC as a representative governance body, and to train personnel to effectively negotiate and fight for intellectual property, commercial, indigenous, cultural and other rights.
- the need to provide mechanisms for information sharing, awareness building, and the creation of networks among the Mansions and individual members of the global Rastafari communities.
- Rastafari culture and cultural expressions are varied, covering a range of creative and heritage issues, but there exists many misunderstandings, and there is no acceptable valuation or mapping of what constitutes Rastafari culture and cultural expressions.
- there is need for the RMC to develop internal capacity, and to engage with professionals in fund management and other business development issues associated with the commercialization of Rastafari culture.
- the resistance of certain members and segments of the Rastafari movement to efforts at collective structured business organization to facilitate the protection of the commercial interests of Rastafari.

- the need to lessen the fragmentation within the movement caused by disunity and infighting among certain prominent members of the Rastafari Movement.

Who or What is Babylon?

The concept of Babylon is a very important aspect of the Rastafari belief system. Babylon is seen as the unjust Western political order inherited from the ancient Roman and Babylonian empires. Babylon in a general sense refers to private and government institutions that are seen by Rastafari as being in opposition to the Rasta belief system. Babylon is also seen as any system that promotes oppression and discrimination, and is often also identified as represented by government, the police and the church. Ministers of the church are regarded as agents for the mental enslavement of Africans and people of African descent. While politicians or "politricksters", are the oppressors of the black race through economic and physical slavery over many centuries. The police are directly called Babylon, as they are seen as the executive agents of Babylon's will. Bob Marley's song "Babylon System" provides some description.[23]

The Rastafarian defiance of Babylon targets both local and international institutions. Defiance is directly connected to the Pope and Rome. Rome itself is sometimes called Babylon, partly because of the 1935 Italian invasion of Ethiopia, and in relation to the Pope being the head of the Roman Catholic Church. The Government of Jamaica is not regarded by Rastafarians as their government, and is seen as the puppet of the British Government and international allies such as the US Government and big multinational corporations.

The Rastafari belief system is by nature radical, and is against the oppression of black people, much of which emanates from the existing economic structures represented and supported by the Babylon system. The language of Rastafari sometimes includes violent expressions. For example, Rasta language admonish sinners to be consumed by fire, oppressors to be smitten, and kings and empires to be overthrown, showing much similarity to the language of the Bible, particularly the Old Testament. Many Christian preachers also use similar violent language, and like Christians, the use of this kind of language by Rastafari does

---

23. https://www.youtube.com/watch?v=J5EoiQX7u5k

not mean they are ready to literally burn people, or fight. This is often misunderstood however.

The defiance of the Babylon system has been an ongoing feature of the development and struggles of Rastafari. The Report of 1960 summarized the situation then as follows:

"The choice before Jamaica is that between social reform which is planned, peaceful and rapid on the one hand, or changes of a different sort. It is certain that Jamaican society cannot continue in its present form. Since economic development presumes social stability, this means that any successful development depends on an intelligent programme of social reform... The general public believes in a stereotype Rastafarian, who wears a beard, avoids work, smokes ganja, and is liable to sudden violence. This type exists, but is a minority. The real danger is that if all Rastafarians are treated as if they are like this, more and more will become extremists."

More than fifty years since the 1960 Rasta Report, the question can still be asked: "To what extent has Jamaica's economic and social development been adversely affected by conflicts between Rastafari and the Babylon system?" Public perceptions and understanding of Rastafari are still flawed and based on misinformation.

Rastafari Culture

Rastafari culture has spread throughout the world, with much impact in communities in the Caribbean, Africa, the Americas and Europe. Rastafari has made a significant contribution to the global popularity of Reggae music, and has also benefited from the acceptance of Reggae in many countries around the world. The doctrines, culture, and lifestyle of Rasta have figured prominently in the lyrical content of Reggae, and have had tremendous influence on the design and presentation of various items of memorabilia, food, clothing and accessories associated with the global Reggae music industry. Any examination of the status of and challenges faced in Reggae music industry development would be grossly inadequate without an examination of the role and impact of Rastafari language, style of dress, religious, cultural and dietary practices.

One of the most significant aspects of Rastafari culture has been the unflinching promotion of the legalization of marijuana, which is used as a sacrament by most Rastas. Rasta Reggae music and artists have for decades promoted the medicinal value of marijuana, long before it became the fashionable position globally. The recent intrusion of big business interests in the commercialization of medicinal and recreational marijuana has resulted in debates about cultural conflicts between Rastafari beliefs and legalized marijuana trading.[24]   There is also concern expressed regarding the implications for Reggae and Reggae artists in Jamaica and a future world of decriminalized and legalized marijuana.[25]

Rasta Language

Original Jamaican Rastafarians are of the opinion that the English language is an imposed colonial language, and that African languages were lost when they were taken into captivity and brought to the West as slaves. In defiance of the system of Babylon, Rastafarians have created a modified vocabulary and dialect. This includes the avoidance of certain words and syllables that are seen as negative, and changing them to positive. One of the most noticeable features of the modified Rastafari vocabulary is the introduction and use of several "I words". In the Rastafari vocabulary the word "I" replaces "me", and the term "I and I" replaces we, and you and I. Many words and phrases commonly used by Rasta have now been embraced in mainstream Jamaican speech.

Rasta Diet and Nutrition

The dietary laws of the Old Testament have greatly influenced what Rastafarians eat. Many Rastas eat very limited types of meat, and do not eat pork or shellfish. Some Rastas eat absolutely no meat, as they regard touching meat as the same as touching death. Eating ital has become a recognized practice. The word ital is derived from the word vital, and the main objective of eating ital is to increase "livity" or the life energy that Rastafari believes lives within all human beings. The general principle of eating ital is that food should be natural, pure, and from the earth. Food which is chemically modified, or contains artificial additives such as colours, flavourings and preservatives are avoided. Some Rastas also avoid salt in foods, especially salt with the addition of iodine. Foods that

24. http://www.vice.com/en_uk/read/marley-natural-betraying-bob-and-jamaica-781

25. http://www.billboard.com/biz/articles/news/legal-and-management/6429593/legalize-it-marijuanas-relationship-with-Reggae-and

have been produced using chemicals such as pesticides and fertilizers are not considered ital.

Many expressions of eating ital include adherence to a strict vegetarian diet. Rastafarian dietary practices are arguably pioneering initiatives in what are now globally accepted as healthy eating habits designed to prevent illness or correct disease. Many Rastas also disapprove of the consumption of alcoholic beverages and the smoking of cigarettes due to the serious health concerns associated with their use.

Rasta/Reggae Branding – Clothing, Accessories, Craft, Services

The colours of the Ethiopian flag (red, gold and green) and the image of the Lion of Judah, which was included in the official Ethiopian flag from 1897 to 1974, have become the most recognizable symbols of Rastafari. Over the years these colours and images have been used globally in the identification and branding of Rasta and Reggae products including clothing, accessories, craft items, restaurants, and events such as music festivals. The Green, Gold and Red colours and the image of the Lion of Judah show the loyalty Rastafari feel towards the Ethiopian state during the reign of Haile Selassie.

Red, black and green are the colours that were used to represent Africa by Marcus Garvey's Universal Negro Improvement Association/UNIA. These colours have also become closely linked to Rastafari and Reggae, and demonstrate the significance of the life and work of Marcus Garvey to the Rastafari and Reggae communities globally. As is the case with the colour combination red, gold, and green, the colour combination red, black and green has also been used over the years in the identification and branding of Rasta and Reggae products and services.

Rastafari and Music

Although the colonial rulers passed laws forbidding what they called "speaking drums" that they believed were used to transmit messages of rebellion, they did allow certain drum and music activity. What was known as Burru or Burra drummers were allowed by slave owners to accompany work songs to encourage labour in the fields and for holiday events such as Christmas celebrations.

Descriptions of seminal Rasta gatherings say the music consisted of singing mostly Revivalist hymns accompanied by rhumba box, tambourine, shakers and sometimes guitars. As Rasta and Burru (Burra) men converged in the slums of West Kingston, Rasta adopted the three set Burru drums and adapted the rhythms. Count Ossie (Oswald Williams), who is credited with creating the Rasta drumming, said that that he was taught by Burru drummer Bro. Job at Salt Lane in West Kingston. In the late 1940s, he contracted Watto King the Burru drummer who taught Bro. Job to play, and himself a master drum maker, to make a set of drums. (Verena Reckord, "Rastafarian Music – An Introductory Study", Jamaica Journal, August 1977, p9). Ossie subsequently spread his style of playing through visits to various Rasta camps in different locations on the island for what became known as grounations (also spelled groundations. As with the Nyabinghi movement of east central Africa, the Jamaican Nyabinghi (grounation) sessions invoked the power of Jah against the oppressors. A typical Rastafari Nyabinghi celebration or grounation includes drumming, chanting, dancing, and the smoking of marijuana. Chanting often includes the recitation of Psalms and variations of well-known Christian hymns.

The rhythms of Nyabinghi eventually became a major influence of popular Ska, Rock Steady and Reggae music in Jamaica, resulting in the emergence of Afro-Caribbean music forms shaped by African, Caribbean, European and American cultures. Some ethnomusicologists make a direct link between the parts played on Rasta Nyabinghi drums and the patterns of the bass and rhythm guitars and the piano chops of Reggae. Count Ossie was the first artist known to have recorded Nyabinghi in Jamaica, on the Folkes Brothers, "Oh Carolina", produced by Prince Buster in 1960.. The Skatalites are also credited with combining parts of Nyabinghi with Jazz to create the music form that became known as Ska.

Recordings by Ras Michael and the Sons of Negus also contributed significantly to the popularity of Nyabinghi music. [26] Many of the exponents of contemporary Reggae music such as Bob Marley, Buju Banton, Luciano, Sizzla, and even American roots Reggae artists such as Groundation, have used Nyabinghi drumming in their recordings. So do many non-Rastas such as Jimmy Cliff and Prince Buster, who are both Muslims. [27]

---

26. https://www.youtube.com/watch?v=JsrZZEjgB2Q
27. https://www.youtube.com/watch?v=mcOtJ9V0BG0

Reggae began to enter international consciousness in the 1970s due to the work of formative exponents such as Jimmy Cliff (The Harder They Come movie and soundtrack), Toots and the Maytals, Desmond Dekker, and Marley. Recording collaborations with international artists Johnny Nash (I Can See Clearly Now, Stir It Up and Guava Jelly – 1972), and Eric Clapton (I Shot The Sheriff – 1974), were ground breaking accomplishments for Reggae. The international awareness about Reggae and Rastafari grew in the 1980s and 1990s as a result of the works of Marley and the Wailers and other Reggae musicians with strong Rastafarian elements in their music, such as Freddie McGregor, Burning Spear, Peter Tosh, Bunny Wailer, Third World, Dennis Brown, Israel Vibration, The Congos, The Abyssinians, Black Uhuru, The Mighty Diamonds, Culture, Big Youth and many others.

In the final decades of the 20th century Rastafari doctrine and Reggae music were spread globally as complementary forces and influences. Lyrical themes highlighting social, political and racial issues caused many marginalized and disadvantaged groups around the world to embrace Reggae and Rastafari. Numerous Reggae and Rastafarian musicians now exist in countries in Africa, the Caribbean, the Americas, and Europe. The emergence of Reggae as a globally accepted music form can be attributed to the combination of African, Caribbean, European and American rhythms, with lyrical content that is influenced by the themes and messages emanating from Rastafari culture and lifestyle. The life and works of Bob Marley have done the most to raise international awareness about Reggae and Rastafari.

At the turn of the century the popularity of roots Rasta Reggae began to wain in Jamaica despite the efforts of artists such as Garnett Silk, Tony Rebel, Capleton, Anthony B, Jah Mason, Luciano, Jah Cure, Richie Spice, Damian Marley, Alborosie, and Morgan Heritage. Since 2010 however there has been a resurgence in the popularity of roots Rasta Reggae inside Jamaica, led by several young artists with deep Rasta-centric musical styles, such as Protoje, Chronixx, Jah9, Kabaka Pyramid, Raging Fyah, Jesse Royal, Kelissa, Iba Mahr and Pentateuch. This resurgence has also gained the attention of international audiences, and has been labeled the Reggae Revival.[28]

While Rastafari and the popularity of Reggae have grown globally,

---

28. https://www.youtube.com/watch?v=LfeIfiiBTf

there is still evidence of discrimination against Rasta and Reggae artists, both inside Jamaica as well as in segments of the international community. Some argue that there are cultural and lifestyle traditions of Rasta that have posed challenges for the development of institutions and business practices necessary for Reggae music industry development. In support of this argument, reference is often made to the success in recent years of home grown Reggae artists from North America and Europe, such as Gentleman from Germany and Matisyahu from the USA, compared to the decline in international business for Jamaican Reggae artists who more closely embrace Rastafari principles in their music and lifestyles.

Many Rastafari elders also hold fast to the view that the Babylon system continues to try to silence the message of Rastafari. One such elder is Ocho Rios based Rastaman and Nyabinghi chanter and drummer Prof I. Below is an excerpt from an interview conducted with Prof I at his home in Jamaica.

Prof I – Rastafari Elder/Nyabinghi Drummer and Chanter

"To do good and to do the right thing is very hard. It is very hard because the people who are at the top, the people who are doing the wrongs, the people who are doing wickedness, they are the ones in power, they are the ones who have the money, they are the ones who can twist and turn things. If they want to keep the people at war with each other, they keep them poor. If you are a slave master and you give all your slaves their own house and their own farm, you become weak. You have nobody to slave for you anymore. In the Reggae business the people who are promoting the music and the people who are putting out the music are few. When they hear someone come speaking the truth, establishing the truth, they will do anything to prevent us from being heard. The people who really want this message of truth to go out there, don't have the power to put it out.

As I see it, Haile Selassie gave InI Reggae music as our food basket, to provide all the things that we need. First Rasta tried farming, but the people would not buy our food. They would steal it. Rasta also started knitting tams and making and selling buttons. Then came Bob Marley with Reggae music. Rastafari is not a business, but Reggae music is a business. It is the food basket for Rasta, and that is what Bob Marley was establishing, even if he was not conscious of it. Sad too say, but I don't think Bob fulfilled all his physical work that he wanted to do, but he fulfilled his work within the words, and word sound is power, and he gave the power to the people. No Reggae artist can now say the things that Bob Marley already said, because he already said it. He set a foundation. All they have to do is build on it. Don't tear it down.

A lot of people don't know where Bob Marley is coming from. Bob Marley is coming from Nyabinghi, and Reggae music is coming from Nyabimghi, but many can't see the foundation. When Bob Marley does Nyabinghi songs they say it is Reggae. "Fly Away Home To Zion" by Bob Marley is Nyabinghi music. Bob did a lot of Nyabinghi songs. Certain types of lyrics do not go with Nyabinghi music. It does not work, because it is a spiritual music. It is a music of upliftment. It is a music to free your mind to travel all over the world. So, if they don't want me to leave here to travel to establish the message, it's no problem, because telepathically and spiritually we are there, and now we have the media.

I know that people are scared to put out Nyabinghi because it is a music of truths and rights, and that is what some people are afraid of. The original Nyabinghi was a warrior and she was also a drummer, and a farmer. Yet in Jamaica the religious Rastas say women can't play drums. I am one who let the women play drums, and that is another fight. If the original Nyabinghi is a woman, why can't a woman play the drum? Queen Nyabinghi took her name when she was fighting against the colonial powers in East Africa. Today they are trying to use Nyabinghi as an organization. Nyabinghi is not an organization. Nyabinghi is the chant, the prayer, and we pray through the mother. That's where Nyabinghi comes from.

There are some brethren trying to register and establish Nyabinghi as an organization, and as a church, but Nyabinghi is not an organization. Rastafari is not about church. Church is religion. Rastafari is not religion. Rastafari is a way of life. It is a spiritual movement. It is not something you can force onto someone by saying Rastafari is right, and that you must be Rasta, and that this is the right way. No, you have to have that spiritual connection with yourself, your ancestors, the ancient ones, the people, the people of righteousness, to come together and get the power. Now that people want to become preachers, leaders and teachers, they try to register, as they want to be accepted by the society. As long as the society accept you, you are not Rasta. Bob Marley said that too. "Me no have no friend in a high society". I think it is the spiritual power that was moving through Bob. It was the power of the almighty.

To the young Rasta artists such as Chronixx, Protoje, and Jah9 I say, keep it real and step it up to another level, because Haile Selassie said we must learn to accept change, and we see change happening. Still you have to maintain that ancient indigenous livity. There was a time I never lived in a house. Now I live in a house. I never drove a car. Now I have a car. So these young artists coming up will put a little flavor in the music and there is no problem with that, as long as they are keeping it real. My advice is, don't let anyone buy and sell you as if you are some item on a shelf. Stand up for what you want, and think about your ancient brethren that died, and Rasta don't deal with death, but they died so that you can be here. What are you going to do with all this money you are going to make? Haile Selassie says, any fool can make money, but it takes a wise man to spend and keep it. That means if you were rich and you become poor, you are a fool.

What these brethren who are making money need to do is put it in the right place, and to me the right place is to educate yourself and feed yourself. So it's agriculture and education. Land is a must. Stop the quarrel about the Government and capture land. You have the American "God", which is "In God We Trust", the money. Take it and buy the land. Give unto Caesar what is due to Caesar. Buy the land. If you want to have power, take their "God" and then they will bow, but use it positively.

So, for all these young artists who are sending out the right words, we need the right livity, because words without works is vain. That is why I live from raw food for over 40 years because that is what I preach. Don't tell I that this is blue and you are living white. To these brethren I say, you have two ears and one mouth. you need to listen more, because you are in the media, you are on the front line and are targets. They have killed all of the leaders. I am not one of them. Haile Selassie is my leader. I don't believe in leader, teacher or preacher, because they are all transgressors. They get the power but take it unto themselves. You need to give the power to the people, because the voice of the people is the voice of the almighty. It's the people that put you there, so what are you doing *for the people? What I try to do is to maintain this ancient indigenous livity of Rastafari. Don't find yourself drinking, smoking, and spouting. Find yourself in the bushes with nature. Talk to the birds and trees, and give thanks if you get an answer. That's the advice I have to give.*

The system was designed and created to keep our children in darkness. The computer, the TV and the Internet have become parents, and we as parents have allowed that. Sometimes when children are giving trouble at home you give them the computer and the TV, and the computer and the TV become their parents. The system keeps you so hungry and so broke that instead of you looking about your children and teaching your children, you are forced to be hustling to put food on the table. As we speak about righteousness, millions of dollars are being spent to keep the children in darkness.

When Bob Marley came with his music youths were thinking positively. When Bob passed they gave the title king to Yellowman, and what was he saying? Bob was telling the people about how to live, how to unite and how to survive; telling them about the black king. Those who run the system do not want that, and figured they had made a mistake by letting Bob through the doors. They were dancing and listening to the "Riddims". They never knew the words were so powerful. When they found out Bob was opening the eyes of the people, enlightening the people about righteousness, love and unity, and knocking down racism, they decided to get rid of those messages, so after Yellowman came Shabba Ranks. There was a time when only Miss Lou[29] could say "gal" in Jamaica. Now nice beautiful women with children are in the dancehall taking their frocks and sweeping the floor. Before you could not call a woman gal, now everybody is a gal. They say music shall teach them a lesson, and music alone shall live, but what type of music.

Bob and myself never went to any big school. Yet we could go to any university and lecture about Rastafari because we did not learn from their system. We learned through our experience. Our knowledge comes from the things that we go through in life. The professors at the universities all read the same book, so they have the same story. They don't live my livity. My livity taught me something different"

---

29. http://en.wikipedia.org/wiki/Louise_Bennett-Coverley

Bob Marley – Rastaman and People's Hero
– *Facebook note – February 19, 2011* [30]

The debate as to whether the Honorable Robert Nesta Marley should be accorded the status of National Hero in Jamaica has been ongoing for many years, and unfortunately many Jamaicans continue to display a propensity to devalue their own.

A hero may be defined as a person distinguished for courage, personal bravery, bold enterprise, or strength of mind to meet or endure adversity. While Jamaicans talk and express opinions as we are known to do, and in fact, should be encouraged to do, it is important to take time to study the life and work of Bob Marley both locally and internationally.

We should ask ourselves a couple of questions. For example, how much has the work and life of Bob Marley contributed to the success of Jamaica's number one   industry, tourism? How much did Bob's musical works contribute to the liberation of the people of Southern Africa and the abolition of apartheid? How much endurance does it take for an almost "fatherless" child from a poor Jamaican community to rise to become one of the wealthiest and most influential individuals in his country, and without doubt the most popular Jamaican and Rastaman worldwide, after spending only 36 years with us in the flesh?

Bob Marley's lyrics demonstrate tremendous courage and personal bravery as he sought to represent and champion the cause of disadvantaged peoples worldwide. His life is also characterized by courage and bravery as exemplified in his efforts at bringing unity between Michael Manley and Edward Seaga, and an end to tribal political warfare in Jamaica through the internationally publicized "Peace Concert" at the National Stadium. His live concert performance in Kingston while bandaged from fresh gunshot wounds after an attempt on his life certainly ranks high as a demonstration of personal bravery and courage.

Bob Marley's life and music must be examined in the context of whom and what he represented. His music represented the voice of a disadvantaged majority in Jamaica, Africa and many other places

30. https://www.facebook.com/notes/lloyd-stanbury/bob-marley-the-rastamans-hero/10150414111865355

around the world. As a result of the very positive influences and impressions created through his music, I am absolutely proud to be identified as a Jamaican wherever I go in the world. Millions of people around the world regard the Honourable Robert Nesta Marley as their hero.

"Emancipate yourselves from mental slavery. None but ourselves can free our minds."- Marcus Garvey/Bob Marley."

Rastafari, Ganja and the Jamaican Government
– Facebook note, February 27, 2014 [31]

Recent publicity regarding the issues surrounding Pinnacle and the legalization of Ganja have brought into full focus the inefficiencies and corruption that characterize government in Jamaica since our so-called independence in 1962.

When one looks at the wealth of natural and human resources that Jamaica has been blessed with, and contrast this with the economic and social development of our beloved nation, one can argue that Jamaica has had the worst government representation of any developing country in the world. I would also take it a step further to conclude that we have no one to blame but ourselves for our failures. We the citizens must accept responsibility as we continue to vote in favor of politicians who promote nepotism, the appointment of party loyalists instead of competent professionals, and a system where ministers of government are appointed strictly on the basis of their popularity and ability to win a seat in the elections.

The handling of the Rastafari debacle regarding Pinnacle speaks volumes. Rastafari culture is revered globally, yet successive Jamaican governments have failed to protect, respect and preserve Pinnacle, the birthplace of Rasta. Instead our governments have persecuted Rasta, discriminated against Rasta, and turned a blind eye to the desecration of Pinnacle, even in the face of local and international protests.

The Pinnacle/Rastafari issue is further compounded when we take into consideration the recent announcements and posturing of various government ministers and their friends regarding the issue

---

31. https://www.facebook.com/notes/lloyd-stanbury/rastafari-ganja-and-jamaican-government/10154386602980355

of Ganja legalization in Jamaica. Pinnacle is recorded in our history as the first commercial Ganja farm in Jamaica, and for decades the Rastafari community has suffered at the hands of the Jamaican government and police force, primarily because of the use of Ganja. Any future government policy position on Ganja MUST include atonement for the abuse inflicted on Rasta for the use of Ganja. In particular, the destruction of the Pinnacle community and incarceration of its leader Leonard Howell, must be addressed.

Pinnacle and Ganja are not just Rastafari issues. Both provide examples of what is wrong with government in Jamaica – incompetent ministers, corruption, nepotism, hypocrisy, and a lack of true appreciation for the value of Jamaica's human and natural resources.

Summary

- Reggae music has played an integral role in the promotion of Rastafari.
- Rastafari doctrine and philosophy have significantly influenced the global popularity of Reggae.
- Rastafari philosophy of resistance to colonial systems and commercial practices regarded as representations of Babylon, have resulted in obstacles to the business development of many Rasta Reggae artists.
- The individualistic nature of Rastafari ironically creates challenges for unity and organization in Reggae music
- Traditional government resistance to Rastafari continues to adversely affect relationships between Reggae artists and representatives of government
- Rastafari language and dietary practices have been spread via Reggae music and become widely accepted globally.
- Rastafari branding, largely associated with Reggae is widely exploited commercially and mainly by non-Jamaicans and non-Rastas.
- Despite its worldwide appeal, Rastafari remains largely misunderstood and misrepresented globally, and many inconsistencies and differences of opinion exist among Rastas.

Reggae in the Diaspora

The migration of people from Africa to the West, and from Jamaica to various countries around the world, are undoubtably signifi- cant contributing factors to the popularity of Reggae. African and Jamaican diasporic communities can justifiably lay claim to having set the foundation for the global appreciation and growth of Reggae music. In this chapter some of these factors are explored so that Reggae market- ers can consider them in their planning.

The African Diaspora and Reggae

A diaspora can be defined as a scattered population with a common origin in a smaller geographic area. The island of Jamaica and the African continent are geographic areas with interesting and connected diasporic experiences.

The African diaspora comprises communities mainly in the Americas, Europe, and the Middle East that have developed from the historic and present day movement of peoples from various African countries. The movement of Africans throughout the world has been both forced and voluntary. Forced movement of Africans occurred through the Atlantic and Arab slave trades which took slaves from Eastern and Central African countries to the Middle East and from West Africa to Europe and the Americas. Voluntary movement of Africans occurred in very small num- bers prior to the beginning of the 20th century with the arrival in the Americas of a few Africans.

At the turn of the 20th century, Africans began to migrate to Europe voluntarily in much greater numbers, creating new diaspora communities that were not connected with the slave trade. The forced movement of Africans to the West during the slave trade, and the call for return to the East and for reparations, have been themes for many popular Reggae recordings. Burning Spear's Slavery Days32 and Capture Land33 by Chronixx provide great examples.

The word Reggae emerged in the 1960s as the description of a musical genre originating in Jamaica. There are various recorded stories of the origins of the word "Reggae", including the association with a 1968 recording by Toots and the Maytals called Do the Reggay. Other reports link the acceptance and popular use of the word to music producer Bunny Lee and Ska/Reggae artist Derrick Morgan. In his book "Catch A Fire – The Life of Bob Marley" author Timothy White states that Bob Marley claimed that the word Reggae came from a Spanish tern meaning "the King's music". Reggae is sometimes used in a broad sense to refer to various types of popular Jamaican music, but is more specifically a description of a genre that evolved out of Ska and Rocksteady.

As discussed in the previous chapter, Rastafari culture has had a very significant influence on the development of Reggae. Nyabinghi rhythms eventually became a major influence of popular Ska, Rock Steady and Reggae music in Jamaica, and made a significant contribution to the shaping of various Afro Caribbean music forms that reflect African, Caribbean, European and American cultures.

African Reggae and Non-African Reggae on the Continent

Reggae music has been popular on the African continent for several decades, and for much the same reason that it is popular around the world—its unique rhythm and sound, and its ability to move people in body, mind and spirit. The music has been spread and developed across the African continent through ongoing musical exchanges between artists from Jamaica and artists from various African countries. In the 1970s music by artists such as Jimmy Cliff and The Wailers became very popular in Africa, and provided a significant source of inspiration and influence to

32. https://www.youtube.com/watch?v=Zv8q0IUSQaU
33. https://www.youtube.com/watch?v=YoHzqwLxk_Y

African musicians in countries such as Ghana, Sierra Leone, Nigeria, and Zimbabwe. Thomas Mapfuma (Zimbabwe), and Sonny Okosun (Nigeria), are two of the earliest proponents of African Reggae who achieved international success. [34]

Bob Marley's performance in Harare at the Zimbabwe independence celebrations in 1980 is regarded by many as the turning point at which Reggae took off throughout Africa. Currently there are African Reggae bands in all regions of the continent, and the influence of the music genre on traditional African music continues. Several African Reggae artists have also risen to international prominence, including Alpha Blondy and Tiken Jah Fakoly from the Ivory Coast, Lucky Dube from South Africa, Rocky Duwani from Ghana, and Majek Fashek from Nigeria.[35] . In more recent years we have witnessed recording artists such as the Sierra Leone Refugee All Stars, the Nigerian acts 2 Face, Asa, and P-Square rise to international prominence through the infusion of Reggae and Dancehall with traditional African music.[36]

Since Marley's performance in Zimbabwe in 1980, the flow of Jamaican artists into Africa for concert performances has continued and grown in recent years. The African music market is now regarded by Jamaican Reggae artists as one of the most important in the world. A very long list of Jamaican artists have visited and continue to perform frequently in African countries such as Kenya, South Africa, Zimbabwe, Ivory Coast, Tanzania, Nigeria, Ghana, Uganda, Ethiopia, and Gambia. In April 2015 there was a major collaboration between Jamaicans and Ivorians to stage the first Abi Reggae Festival and Conference in Abidjan, Ivory Coast. Several West African and Jamaican Reggae artists participated in the event, which also had Dr. Julius Garvey, son of Marcus Garvey, as a special invited guest.[37]

The creative impact of Reggae in Africa has manifested itself in three ways:

1. The emergence of home-grown African Reggae by artists who have stuck to the original roots music traditions of Jamaican Reggae.

34. https://www.youtube.com/watch?v=pGXSNVOQ53Q
35. https://www.youtube.com/watch?v=IxE8XZ3Kvcg
36. https://www.youtube.com/watch?v=HlobCyXn2_o
37. http://jamaica-gleaner.com/article/entertainment/20150422/abi-Reggae-festival-ivory-coast-success

Lucky Dube provides an example. [38]
2. The fusion of traditional Reggae music styles with traditional African music, as exemplified is some recordings by Alpha Blondy.[39]
3. The emergence of African Dancehall/Rap music styles produced and presented by younger musicians and music producers across the continent, such as Nigerian recording stars P-Square.[40]

Reggae's popularity in Africa should not be attributed solely to the creative and cultural exchanges experienced through travel by artists between Africa, Jamaica and Europe. There are also very important historical connections between the Rastafari movement and East African countries such as Kenya, Uganda and Tanzania that could explain the wide-scale acceptance and popularity of Reggae in these countries. The impact of Kenya on Reggae music and Rastafari can be traced to the Mau Mau uprising and military conflicts that occurred in Kenya between 1952 and 1960. As Jamaican anti-colonial youth and their Kenyan counterparts resisted the same British rulers, media images in the 1950s of the dreadlocked Mau Mau warriors reinforced the rebel efficacy of the long uncombed hair style that members of two strident West Kingston Rasta groups, Youth Black Faith and Higes Knots, had begun wearing in the late 1940s (Chevannes, Barry. "Enter the Dreadlocks". Rastafari: Roots and Ideology. Syracuse University Press, 1994. p169). The Mau Mau revolutionaries were primarily young men and women of the Kikuyu group, who decided that they would not cut their hair until Kenya was liberated from white colonial settlers. It is said that photos of these long haired men and women with locks reached Jamaica, and that members of the Rastafari community quickly embraced the appearance of the Kenyan Mau Mau freedom fighters. The Kikuyu are the largest ethnic group in Kenya, and their influence in government and the economic and social development of Kenya is very significant.

The historical influences between the Mau Mau, Rastafari, and Reggae, as well as the close friendship between former Jamaican Prime Minister Michael Manley and Jomo Kenyatta (regarded as the founding father of the Kenyan nation), probably explains why Kenya is the African

38. https://www.youtube.com/watch?v=R0B6BhwpR3w
39. https://www.youtube.com/watch?v=-tFBulAJar8
40. https://www.youtube.com/watch?v=ttdU19Kwce8

country where Reggae is most popular. The Kenya/Reggae connection is also exemplified in the common use and reverence accorded to names such as Uhuru, as in Black Uhuru, and Uhuru Kenyatta, (son of Jomo Kenyatta and the 4th President of Kenya), as well as the use of names associated with Reggae and Rastafari, such as Haile Selassie, and Marcus Garvey, in the naming for streets in Nairobi. Jomo Kenyatta is also referred to as the Burning Spear, the name later embraced by the famous Rasta Reggae artist Winston "Burning Spear" Rodney.

As outlined previously in this chapter, early Rastafari came under the influence of the rituals of the Nyabinghi movement of east central Africa—Rwanda, Uganda and Tanzania. The Nyabinghi expressions of Rastafarians in Jamaica—the ritual chanting and drumming have been credited as the main creative influences in the shaping of Jamaican Ska, Rock Steady and Reggae. Consequently, Reggae's acceptance and popularity in Uganda and Tanzania is also deep rooted and wide-spread.

Reggae and Africans in the Americas

The socio-political impact of Reggae and Jamaican artists on the African American community in the USA provides an interesting case study. On his historic visit to Jamaica in April 2015, Barack Obama, the first African American President of the USA, visited the Bob Marley Museum as his first stop on his overnight stay. While at the museum he declared that he had all Bob's albums, and that he has been a big fan since being a high school student.[41] Obama's visit to Jamaica also resulted in a firestorm of controversy, as Jamaica's leading young Rasta artist Chronixx was publicly very critical of the failure of the government of the USA to exonerate Marcus Garvey, who was charged and convicted in the United States of mail fraud in 1923. Marcus Garvey is not only revered by the Rastafari community, he is also seen as a mentor and source of inspiration for African American civil rights leaders such as Martin Luther King, and Malcolm X, who paved the way for Obama to become President. Jamaican American recording artist Harry Belafonte has also made a huge contribution to the American civil rights movement.[42]

In the Americas, the coming together of diverse groups from around

---

41. http://www.washingtonpost.com/blogs/post-politics/wp/2015/04/08/obama-makes-a-night-time-visit-to-bob-marley-museum/

42. https://www.youtube.com/watch?x-yt-ts=1422411861&v=y7kmTGhkB-w&x-yt-cl=84924572

the world has resulted in the creation of multi-ethnic societies. In Central America, South America, and the Caribbean, most societies are descendants with European, American Indian, and African ancestry. Similar multi-ethnic societies have also developed in North America. These multi-ethnic communities have significantly influenced cultural output and the appreciation of diverse cultures. One manifestation of this is the common thread of rhythms of Africa evident in music originating from the Caribbean, North, Central and South America. Some African descendants in the diaspora have kept their ties to the African continent, thus creating a global community with common cultural and family values, as well as spiritual beliefs.

Politics, Religion, Economics and Reggae in Africa

The religious, political, and economic implications of Reggae's penetration and acceptance in Africa are far-reaching and complex. Political struggles, religious differences, high levels of music piracy, and the digital divide, are all very significant aspects of African life that have impacted or been affected by Reggae music's presence on the continent.

Reggae in African Politics

Reggae music has been loosely referred to by many as the soundtrack to African liberation[43]. The very close association between Reggae artists and the Rastafari culture of resistance against colonial domination, enabled the recording and promotion of a music deeply steeped in political protest. The ongoing disenfranchisement of Rastafari from the means of production and wealth in Jamaica resulted in Rastas being at the forefront in contesting institutionalized racism and classism inherited from colonial systems of government around the world and in Africa in particular. Rastafari look to Africa as the source of their ancestry and identity, and use Reggae music as a form of protest against oppressive social conditions.

As a result of the prophecies of Marcus Garvey, and the teachings of

---

43. Sakufi-Rumongi Kagenza. "Rwanda: Reggae Music - a Soundtrack to African Liberation". January 03, 2013 http://www.newtimes.co.rw/section/article/2013-01-03/61468/

The article in "The New Times" (Rwanda) online lists Bob Marley, Burning Spear or Joseph Hill, the Mighty Diamonds, Wailing Souls, the Gladiators, Dennis Brown, Don Carlos, I Jah Man Levi, Freddie McGregor and John Holt, as "a few of the prominent Reggae musicians and bands that have produced a rich soundtrack to the African liberation struggle."

Leonard Howell, Rastafari in Jamaica became focused on Haile Selassie, as well as on Ethiopia as important symbols of Africa. Africa as a whole also gained the attention and interest of Rastafarians and Reggae musicians. The mantra of Rastafari and many Reggae artists is "Africa and Africans must be free". The Reggae messages of liberation and resistance against domination and discrimination by colonial and post-colonial systems of government found root and relevance across Africa and in particular in countries such as Angola, Rhodesia (now Zimbabwe), and South Africa.

The independence wars against Portugal in Angola and Mozambique in the 1970s, and the independence of Zimbabwe from Britain in 1980, were all the focus and subject of Reggae recordings and performances. There have also been reports of Reggae music being used as motivation for freedom fighters and protestors in liberation movements for independence in other African countries.

The struggles in South Africa against apartheid and for the release of Nelson Mandela became especially symbolic as decolonization throughout Africa continued to spread. Reggae music's identification with the anti-apartheid and free Nelson Mandela movements cannot be overstated. One of the earliest anti-apartheid songs on record is Apartheid by Peter Tosh, done in 1977.[44] The list of Reggae recordings and concert events that were promoted in support of the anti-apartheid and free Mandela movements is a very long one, and includes performances and recordings in the 1970s and 1980s by Bob Marley, Peter Tosh, Third World, Burning Spear, the Mighty Diamonds, the Abyssinians, Carlene Davis, Eddy Grant, and many more. After Mandela's release from prison in 1990, several Reggae songs were also recorded that commented on and celebrated his release and later in his presidency, such as Shepherd Be Careful by Dennis Brown and Cocoa T.[45]

Reggae and Religion in Africa

Religious activity in Africa varies from country to country, and within each country. African religious practices also have a very significant influence on art, culture, and politics. The inhabitants of Africa are mainly adherents to Christianity, Islam, or traditional African religions. The vast

---

44. https://www.youtube.com/watch?v=3_8bWsee0I0
45. https://www.youtube.com/watch?v=xeUYHwWAIoE

majority are either Muslims or Christians, and there is a great degree of merger between the different beliefs of Islam, Christianity and traditional African religions. According to the USA published World Book Encyclopedia, Islam is the largest religion in Africa, with 47 percent of the continent's population being Muslim. This is followed closely by Christianity. Despite there being some degree of interaction and tolerance among Muslims, Christians and persons in traditional African religions, there still exists significant differences in beliefs, traditions, social norms and aspirations, that have resulted in continued religious and political conflicts.

Founding Rastafarian leaders in Jamaica focused on a reinterpretation of Christianity and the Bible, and distanced themselves from Islam, and traditional African religions and practices such as Voodoo, and Obeah. The identification of Rastafari by many Africans as a Christianity influenced religious movement, and its association with Reggae music, has in some instances resulted in the rejection of Reggae by Africans of the Muslim faith.

Despite the historical connections between Reggae, Rastafari, Africa's Mau Mau revolutionaries, and the Nyabinghi resistance movement in East Africa, Reggae and Rastafari are in some instances regarded negatively as foreign influences from Jamaica. There continues to be a significant degree of misunderstanding in some African countries regarding the Rastafari belief system.

The Economics of Reggae in Africa

Most African countries experience extremely high levels of music piracy when compared to countries in Western Europe and the Americas. Securing legitimate sales of all genres of recorded music, including Reggae, is a major challenge throughout Africa. The business of music is also conducted at a very informal level throughout Africa, with the exception of segments of the South African music industry. Understanding and appreciation of the value of intellectual property rights are at a very low level in most African countries. The digital divide, evident from the low levels of Internet penetration and use, and inaccessibility to other new and emerging technologies, makes it very difficult for the recording industry in Africa to adjust to the new music business models that drive industry growth.

As far as live music in Africa is concerned, the popularity and wide scale acceptance of Reggae has resulted in a growing sector with the staging of music festivals and concerts that feature local African, Jamaican and other international Reggae performers. Several African Reggae artists have emerged and become viable international live music entities.

As a region, Africa does provide the most receptive and largest potential audience for both recorded and live Reggae music. The very low levels of professionalism within the music industries of the majority of African countries, and the slow pace of adaptation to new technologies must however be addressed if this very large and receptive Reggae audience is to become a legitimate commercial market for music products and services.

The African Union describes the African diaspora as made up of people of African origin living outside the continent, who are willing to contribute to the development of the continent and the building of the African Union, irrespective of their citizenship and nationality. The Constitutive Act of the African Union states that it shall "invite and encourage the full participation of the African diaspora as an important part of our continent, in the building of the African Union." - These sentiments are reflected in the music of Bob Marley, Africa Unite,[46] and Peter Tosh, African [47]. The economic viability of Reggae on the African continent is closely tied to the need for African unity and the development of stronger links between Africans at home and those in the diaspora.

The Afro-Jamaican Diaspora and Reggae

The Jamaican diaspora comprises people who voluntarily left Jamaica to work and live overseas. Jamaicans can be found all over the world, and may probably be the most widely dispersed people of any small island nation. The largest pockets of persons of Jamaican origin outside of Jamaica exist in the United States, the United Kingdom, Canada, other Caribbean islands, and across the Caribbean coast of Central America. Estimates are that over 2 million Jamaicans reside outside of Jamaica. It is often said that just as many Jamaicans live outside Jamaica as those that live on the Island. The value and importance of migrant Jamaicans to the social and economic development of Jamaica is not sufficiently

---

46. https://www.youtube.com/watch?v=FpfxD0yY6f8
47. https://www.youtube.com/watch?v=dMRGmJjbtzw

recognized by domestic government policy in the opinion of many. With the exception of a recent Diaspora Mapping Initiative launched within the Jamaican Ministry of Foreign Affairs, very little meaningful policies or activities exist. [48]

However, an active Diaspora movement has been growing since 2004, when the Government of Jamaica and the Jamaican private sector invited more than 250 people living abroad to convene the first Jamaican Diaspora Conference. Since then there have been biennial meetings and a Jamaican Diaspora Foundation (JADF) was established and the Jamaica Diaspora Institute (JDI), its operating arm, has been located in the Mona School of Business and Management at the University of the West Indies, Mona Campus. The JADF website says its principal goal is "strengthening the engagement of persons and groups in the Jamaican Diaspora in Jamaica's development," and that this will be achieved through collaboration with the government, businesses and non-governmental organizations in Jamaica.[49]

Jamaican migration to other countries commenced around the middle of the 19th century with the movement of labourers into Panama, Costa Rica and the United States. Both the United States and the United Kingdom recruited labourers from Jamaica during World Wars I and II. The post-World War II reconstruction in the United Kingdom resulted in high levels of migration from Jamaica. Migration trends from Jamaica changed significantly in the post- independence period with regulatory changes after 1962. More stringent immigration laws in the United Kingdom after Jamaica's independence, coincided with new policies in the USA and Canada that made education and skills more important determinants for migration than nationality and race. From the 1960s onwards the USA became the main destination for skilled migrants from Jamaica.

As is the case with African migration, Jamaicans in the diaspora have taken with them their cultural, spiritual and family values and beliefs. Jamaica's strong links to Africa through Rastafari and Reggae have also resulted in significant cultural interplay between the members of the African diaspora and members of the Jamaican diaspora. The two largest areas of concentration of Jamaicans in the diaspora are London and

---

48. http://www.mapjadiaspora.iom.int
49. http://jamaicadiasporaconnect.com/about-us

surrounding cities, and New York and surrounding cities. These areas also have large concentrations of migrants from the African continent. London and New York are also regarded as two of the most important cities in the world for the development and global marketing of popular music, thus providing fertile ground for nurturing Reggae and other music genres that appeal to people of African origin. Harry Belafonte's musical experiences and life story are very instructive in this regard. [50]

Despite the existence of deep cultural and historic ties within the Jamaican and African diasporas, there is still a great deal of disconnect between Jamaicans and their African ancestry. This has been fueled and sustained by an educational system inherited from colonial Great Britain that was designed to keep slaves and ex-slaves controlled. The eradication of the cultural and spiritual roots of the Africans in the West, and the introduction of British and other European cultural practices, was, and still is a feature of the Jamaican, Caribbean and American educational systems. The ignorance of Jamaicans and other African descendants in the West about Africa and their African ancestry is astonishing and contributes to the barriers to meaningful collaboration in music between Jamaica and Africa.

Africans and people of African descent in the Caribbean have also found themselves in a space where access to new and emerging digital technology has been relatively limited and more expensive than is the case in the larger more developed music markets of North America and Western Europe. In light of the tremendous impact on the production, promotion and presentation of music and entertainment content caused by digitization, the Internet and mobile communication trends, failure to address the technology access and training needs of Jamaican and African music industry operators, will prove to be one of the largest barriers to growth of Reggae business throughout the African Diaspora.

Summary

- The large and widely dispersed Jamaican diasporic community has contributed significantly to the global popularity and acceptance of Reggae. However, much has not been done to strategically capitalize on this popularity to grow and tap into the global market for Reggae.
- The acknowledgement of Reggae music as a key promoter of African

---

50. https://www.youtube.com/watch?x-yt-ts=1422411861&v=y7kmTGhkB-w&x-yt-cl=84924572

unity and African liberation by Africans at home and in the African diaspora, has contributed greatly to global popularity of Reggae.

- The African continent represents the largest group of persons in the world who have embraced Reggae music. Africa is potentially the biggest market for Jamaican music..
- The connections between Reggae and Africa are founded in deep historical and socio-political links between Jamaica and several African countries.
- The implications of the connection between Reggae and the teachings and philosophies of Marcus Garvey on economic development, should be more closely examined in any exercise aimed at the expansion of international commercial activity in Reggae music.

The Reggae and Dancehall Debate

There has been a long running debate among musicians and the buying public about what distinguishes traditional Reggae music from dancehall. There are those who say dancehall is Reggae, and others who argue it is an offshoot. The debate even extends to the lyrical content of both types of music, with dancehall detractors decrying a general departure from what they see as the conscious lyrics of Reggae, towards the more sexual and violent tones of dancehall. There are also some who use the term Reggae to define all forms of popular Jamaican music for marketing purposes. It is important for Reggae producers to know and differentiate their product for various market segments and channels.

What is Reggae Music?

The definition of Reggae music requires consideration of a variety of creative and stylistic characteristics, as well as the opinions of the musicians and music producers involved in the process of evolution of Jamaican popular music. Below are some definitions and considerations worthy of note:

Merriam-Webster Dictionary – Reggae is a popular music of Jamaican origin that combines native styles with elements of rock and soul music and is performed at moderate tempos with accent on the offbeat.

All About Jazz (2009 - 10 - 01). Various Artists | Rocksteady: The Roots of Reggae – One of the most easily recognized elements is offbeat rhythms; staccato chords played by a guitar or piano (or both) on the offbeats of the measure. The tempo of Reggae is usually slower than ska and rocksteady.

Cleveland "Clevie" Browne – Although there are exceptions to Reggae's rhythmic rule, most Reggae recordings utilize a pattern known as 'one drop'. The once drop beat is typically a single 4/4 bar of music where the drummer places emphasis on the second and fourth beats of the bar. The emphasis is usually played simultaneously on the kick and snare drums, with the snare beat played on the metal tuning edge of the drum in a style known to drummers as 'rim shot'. In a typical Reggae beat, the Hi-Hat cymbals complement the groove with 8th or 16th notes. The rhythm section (typically piano or guitar), plays a simultaneous up beat riff, often complemented by a shuffle style organ bubble, while sub-frequency bass adds the hypnotic touch. THIS IS REGGAE MUSIC."

What is clear from most definitions of Reggae is that it is of Jamaican origin, it is born out of the infusion of various musical influences, from traditional Caribbean folk music, to African, Latin American, and North American genres. At the root of it all is the distinct Rasta drumming that provides a pattern for the bass, rhythm and piano chops of the tracks. There is a distinctive off-beat element to Reggae. Because of the wide global recognition and exposure of Reggae in the 1970s that was fueled by songs addressing social and political issues, such as apartheid, discrimination, racism, materialism, and the Rastafari movement, Reggae has been widely identified as "protest music". There are, however, other lyrical themes identified with Reggae that relate to personal issues, such as love, having fun and socializing.

Defining Dancehall

The word Dancehall when used in the context of Jamaican music can be traced to the late 1940s. It is derived from the two words dance hall, which were used to describe the venues in which popular Jamaican recordings were played by local sound systems. Throughout the 1950s and 1960s dance hall venues became popular in several inner city communities of Kingston and St. Andrew. The unique Jamaican sound system phenomenon also rose to prominence around the same time, and provided an outlet for the promotion of local music that was not getting exposure from traditional Jamaican radio. The first Jamaican sound systems were mobile high-powered home-made audio systems that were moved from place to place and used to play popular American Rhythm and Blues, as well as Jamaican Ska and Rock Steady recordings.

Sound systems and dance halls catered mainly to younger audiences from lower income communities who were not able to attend the uptown parties. Competition between sound system operators was fierce, and events often attracted large numbers of patrons. The Jamaican sound system phenomenon gave rise to several famous operators and systems, most notable among the pioneers being Clement "Coxsone" Dodd, and Duke Reid. The competition between sound system operators and dance hall venues often led to their association with "Rude Boys" engaged to break up or disturb a competitor's dance. This activity fostered the growth of the violent tendencies of this subculture, and the trend towards competition as against cooperation among persons providing musical entertainment. Dance halls contributed significantly to the rise and popularity of Ska as the earliest primary form of popular music in Jamaica, and heralded the birth of Ska dancing.

It is from the sound system culture that emerged the phenomenon of DJ toasting and unique dub versions of recordings. While early DJs like Count Machuki and King Stitt mainly lauded their own sound systems, their successors such as U Roy and Big Youth emphasized chants with lyrical content of resistance to injustice and the glorification of Rastafari, or songs of romantic love and less stressful aspects of living.

The use of the term dance hall has evolved and has been impacted by cultural and technological changes in Jamaica, eventually giving rise to the single word Dancehall, which is widely used today to describe a sub-genre of Reggae. Music historians have reported that social and political changes that occurred in Jamaica in the 1980s also impacted the lyrical content of locally produced music. The result was a gradual shift away from the more internationally oriented roots Reggae which was fueled by social commentary, towards a music style geared more towards local consumption and with greater emphasis on dancing, sex, violence, and materialism.

In the late 1970s and early 1980s digital/computerized music production was introduced to the music recording studios of Kingston. Prime examples of the use of computerized drum machines include Bob Marley's mid 1970s recording *So Jah Seh*, and Blood Fire Posse's *Rub* a *Dub Soldier* which was recorded in the very early 1980s. It was however the recording of *Under Me Sleng Teng* by Noel Davey and Wayne Smith at King Jammys studio in 1985 that signaled the arrival of digital "riddims"[51].

Steely and Clevie, who would later rise to prominence as the leading Dancehall session musicians and music producers, also experimented in the early 1980s with the use of drum machines and synthesizers. They are credited as being the pioneers of digital/computerized programming and recording of the rhythms that have come to define what is today often referred to as the Dancehall sub-genre of Reggae. Clevie defines Dancehall as follows:

"Dancehall is Jamaican dance music where the rhythms, vocals and mixes are embellished with a positive forceful attitude, and with emphasis on a syncopated two-bar musical pattern. Dancehall recordings are typically made from programmed rhythms with the use of digital/computer technology."

Dancehall culture and sound systems have had a very significant impact on the global popular music scene. Sound systems were brought to the UK in the 1960s and 1970s with the mass migration of Jamaicans, and gave rise to several popular home-grown UK systems such as Jah Shaka, Saxon International, and Aba Shanti-I. Jamaican sound systems are also regarded as the incubators that resulted in the creation of hip-hop through the work of DJ Kool Herc, a Kingstonian who migrated to New York in the 1960s. Kool Herc became very popular in the Bronx and surrounding communities in the 1970s by playing his sound system the Herculords, and the introduction of toasting/rapping to break beats. Pioneering hip-hop stars Grand Master Flash and Afrika Bambaataa are reported to have used Kool Herc's style of deejaying in their initial recordings and performances.

Dancehall music's international success has transcended the breakthrough works of Jamaican artists such as Shabba Ranks, Chaka Demus and Pliers, Shaggy and Sean Paul, to include recordings by non-Jamaicans. Rihanna's Pon De Replay, Christina Aguilera's Woohoo, and Beyonce's Baby Boy (featuring Sean Paul), are examples.[52] Jamaican dancehall beats have also spawned a whole new genre of music called

---

51. https://www.youtube.com/watch?v=Wjw7m-BKmQ8

52. https://www.youtube.com/watch?v=oEauWw9ZGrA

Reggaeton that originated in Panama and was popularized by Puerto Rican artists. Reggaeton has spread to become mainstream popular music in many countries in Central and South America. It is also extremely popular among Latinos in North America. Puerto Rican Don Omar is one of the most famous exponents of Reggaeton.[53]

The concept of Jamaican styled mobile high-powered sound systems has spread to almost every country in the world, with thousands of sound systems now in existence. The competitive nature of the sound system business also continues to include sound clashes between systems, and international sound system competitions. Competition in Dancehall also includes lyrical battles between artists, both on recordings as well as in live stage presentations. The annual stage show, Sting, which is dubbed "The Greatest One-Night Reggae/Dancehall Show on Earth", has been staged consistently in Kingston since 1983, and is arguably the premier live dancehall event in the world. The main feature of Sting is the presentation of on-stage clashes between artists. Over the years several of the clashes staged at Sting have caused controversy, due to the unbridled display of violent and sexually explicit lyrics that often accompany the performances. The 2013 Sting performance clash between Lady Saw and Macka Diamond provides a perfect example. [54]

Dancehall Versus Reggae

There have been many interesting debates with regard to what actually constitutes Dancehall music, what the differences between Dancehall and Reggae are, and whether Dancehall is a separate music genre, a subgenre of Reggae, or just another type of Reggae. Dancehall versus Reggae discussions have even fueled perceptions of a threat to deliberately or inadvertently undermine the progress of traditional roots Reggae music. In March 2009 the New York based Coalition to Preserve Reggae Music (CPR) posed the following question at a community forum and panel discussion carried live on its weekly radio programme: *"Could Dancehall be the Ruination of Reggae?"* According to its official website, the CPR is a charitable organization established to bring Reggae lovers together to work to preserve the art form and its traditional message of healing and

---

53. https://www.youtube.com/watch?v=SMM1WhmIQzI
54. https://www.youtube.com/watch?v=rOCN2nOzoro

unity. In recent years the annual Rebel Salute roots Reggae festival in Jamaica has used the tag line "The Preservation of Reggae".

Within the context of the global music industry, the differences, if any, between Dancehall music and Reggae music should be examined from the following perspectives:

- musical creativity,
- lyrical themes and messages, and
- market access.

Musical Creativity in Dancehall and Reggae

As previously mentioned, Steely and Clevie are recognized as the studio session musicians and music producers who systematically and consistently experimented and recorded the vast majority of Dancehall rhythms between the mid-1980s and early 1990s. They are considered the true pioneers of the Dancehall beat. According to Clevie, Dancehall is a culture and music associated with the Jamaican dance halls. He describes it as Jamaican dance music with a predominant 'clave' accent, wherein the rhythms, vocals and mixes are embellished with a positive forceful attitude. The 'clave', which is a syncopated two-bar musical pattern is predominant in some Afro-Cuban music, such as Rumba and Son. The pattern can also be heard in Bossa Nova, Mento, and some Calypso rhythms, and its roots may be traced to West Africa.

Clevie explains further: "Dancehall recordings are mainly programmed utilizing computer/digital technology, whereas Reggae recordings are largely analogue electric and/or acoustic based."

While there are some clear and distinctive artistic and technical features about Dancehall recordings when compared with Reggae recordings, there are many examples of fusion between the two. Artists such as Barrington Levy, Buju Banton, Sizzla, Shaggy and Chronixx often cleverly fuse Reggae with Dancehall. Examples of recordings incorporating this fusion include One Blood by Junior Reid[55] and All that she Wants by Swedish group Ace of Base.[56] Live music presentations also provide additional examples of the creative differences between Dancehall music and Reggae music. Live Dancehall performances tend to be more reliant

---

55. https://www.youtube.com/watch?v=mnIl1kiShfY
56. https://www.youtube.com/watch?v=8OB28fTKSds

on computerized, digital and other technological support in presentation, such as pre-recorded music tracks and play-back equipment. Live Reggae on the other hand is typically presented with accompanying musicians. There is however much evidence of a mixed approach in the live presentation of Dancehall and Reggae.

Lyrical Themes and Messages

A comparison between Reggae and Dancehall music would not be appropriate without examining the differences in the lyrical themes and messages they project. While both Reggae and Dancehall lyrics cover a wide range of topics, the lyrics in many Reggae songs attempt to raise the political consciousness of the audience, by criticizing materialism, or by informing the listener about controversial subjects such as Apartheid, discrimination, human rights, or police brutality. It is also very common to find Reggae songs that promote the use of marijuana, and advocate for its legalization. Reggae songs and artists also often utilize religious themes, in discussing specific topics, or in giving praise to God (JAH). On the contrary popular Dancehall lyrics have highlighted gun violence, sex, homophobia, and materialism.

According to Louis Chude-Sokei, ("Post-Nationalist Geographies: Rasta, Ragga, and Reinventing Africa "), the realities of life in urban Kingston, New York, London, and Toronto resulted in a shift in attention from global and continental struggles, to describing life in one's neighbourhood. It is also argued that during the rise of Dancehall in the 1980s and 1990s, hopes for a united Africa became much less of a theme for inspiration among the artists.

Both Reggae and Dancehall have had a history of songs with violent gun lyrics. Within the Reggae genre, recordings such as Peter Tosh's *Coming in Hot* and Bob Marley's *I Shot the Sheriff* come to mind. The gun-fighter outlaw image has always been present in Reggae, and many artists in the 1970s and 1980s even adopted the names of Western gun-fighters such as Lone Ranger, Dillinger, John Wayne and Clint Eastwood. The Dancehall genre has produced numerous songs with lyrics portraying gun violence, and the rise of Dancehall music also coincided with the rise in crime and violence in Jamaica in the 1980s and 1990s. Dancehall music with gun lyrics both reflected and promoted the violence on the streets, but in some instances gun lyrics were also used figuratively. The responses from the public to Reggae with gun lyrics and gun lyrics in Dancehall have been varied. Some claim that Dancehall gun lyrics have a tendency to glorify the violent situations that exists in inner city communities, while Reggae gun lyrics seek to address the taking up of arms to fight against reprehensible, discriminatory, and oppressive conditions.

There has been some convergence in the lyrical messages of Reggae and Dancehall music with the emergence of artists such as Buju Banton, Capleton and Sizzla Kalonji, who have embraced Rastafari and introduced elements of Rasta philosophy and lifestyle to their Dancehall recordings.

Market Accessibility of Reggae and Dancehall

The markets for Reggae and Dancehall music are diverse. Popularity and demand are dependent on a number of factors, including traditional and new media promotion, compatibility with other non-Jamaican music formats, and the receptiveness and appreciation of the lyrical content by prospective non-Jamaican audiences. Traditional Jamaican Reggae and its close association with the Rastafari movement and Africa gave rise to a music with globally accepted and appreciated messages that spoke to issues such as equal rights and justice, discrimination, praise to God (JAH), the legalization of marijuana, African liberation and unity, and peace and love between all races. These themes strike a chord with a wide cross section of people around the world who share the sentiments expressed, and results in Reggae being one of the most widely appreciated music genres in the world. Traditional roots Reggae enjoys high levels of respect and appreciation in many countries in the Caribbean, Europe, Africa, South America, and sections of North America.

The Jamaican Dancehall message has been predominantly focused on domestic issues, with much emphasis placed on sex, crime and violence, homophobia, and in more recent times subjects such as skin bleaching and demons. It can be argued that, whereas traditional roots Reggae represents global issues, most Dancehall songs speak more directly to Jamaican inner city life, which holds very little significance to persons outside local communities and the ethnic Caribbean communities of North America and the UK.

The apparent limitation in the global appreciation of Dancehall messages has not prevented the music from being embraced by many non-Jamaican artists in the USA, Europe, Africa, and Latin America. The rise of Reggaeton in Latin America and parts of the USA is a direct result of the incorporation of Jamaican Dancehall beats with Spanish lyrics, vocal styling and instrumentation. Many international artists have also had significant success at the mainstream level in their respective countries with Dancehall, or Dancehall influenced recordings. These include Samy Deluxe from Germany, Million Stylez from Sweden, American artists such as Beyonce, Rihanna, Christina Aguilera, Nicki Minaj, and 2Face Idibia and P-Square from Nigeria. [57]

Socio-Political Considerations Regarding Reggae and Dancehall

The socio-political significance of Reggae and Dancehall at the domestic and international levels makes for a very interesting study. Many theories have been offered over the years by both Jamaican and international academics and music experts. A careful examination of the many studies and reports written provides evidence of interplay in the development of both music forms with Jamaican and international socio-political conditions.

The evolution of Reggae was significantly linked to the Rastafari movement, and that music was also used as an effective vehicle to address issues of concern to the majority of oppressed and disenfranchised poor Jamaicans. The promotion of marijuana use and calls for its legalization, the highlighting of corruption and abuse of power by colonial and post-colonial government administrations, and the targeting of the police as adversarial agents of the Babylon system, have been common themes in Reggae. Reggae and Rastafari is perceived as a threat to the status quo of the local ruling class and political establishment in Jamaica. Several confrontations between the police and members of the Rastafari community, including Reggae artists, have been documented, particularly in the 1950s, 60s and 70s, and still occur today.

In 1972 Michael Manley became Prime Minister of Jamaica and enjoyed very high levels of popularity at home and abroad, particularly in developing countries in Africa, the Caribbean and Latin America. Manley was one of the first Jamaican political leaders to embrace Reggae, as he reached out for the support of the masses. He developed close ties with leading Reggae artists, some of whom performed on his campaign

---

57. https://www.youtube.com/watch?v=_3mHMWO_-mM

stages and recorded songs that were used in support of his philosophies about self-determination. Manley's policy of Democratic Socialism and his close friendship with Fidel Castro were regarded as enablers for the spread of communism in developing countries. It is reported that in the 1970s policy makers in the United States, including   directors of the CIA, were responsible for orchestrating a drive to destabilize the Manley government. This marked the escalation of political and gang violence in Jamaica between supporters of Manley's Peoples National Party (PNP), and supporters of the Jamaica Labour Party (JLP), then led by Edward Seaga.

Two of the most significant concert performances by Bob Marley in Jamaica occurred during this time. They were the "Smile Jamaica" concert, done two days after he was shot, and the "One Love Peace Concert", where he invited both Manley and Seaga on stage to hold hands as a signal to the people of peace, unity, and one love.

Since 2009 Jamaica has experienced a resurgence and renewed popularity in traditional roots Reggae, which has been branded as the Reggae Revival. Many of the artists associated with this resurgence are from middle class backgrounds with a relatively higher level of education than is customary among Jamaican popular musicians. They are also closely associated with trained musicians and visual artists from the Edna Manley College of the visual and performing arts, and have collectively and individually demonstrated their capacity to utilize new technologies and social media to promote their music.

Almost simultaneously with the roots Reggae resurgence, several prominent Jamaican Dancehall artists have experienced career setbacks ranging from criminal charges and imprisonment, to the revocation of travel visas to the USA, fueling an even more vigorous Dancehall versus Reggae debate. The Dancehall versus Reggae debate, and the violent and materialistic stigma attached to Dancehall music, have proven to be distractions that encourage disunity and hamper the further development of the business of music in Jamaica. References are often made to the promotion of aggressive competition between artists, onstage verbal clashes, and the association with violence now identified as a feature of the major Jamaican dancehall concert event, Sting. This is contrasted with the united front that roots artists associated with the Reggae Revival have projected.

The overwhelming majority view of Jamaicans is that the promotion of cooperation and unity among artists will be more productive in a society already plagued by conflict and violence. [58]

What Is Dancehall?
– Facebook note, March 16, 2010[59]

In recent weeks I have been exposed to a number of Internet and newspaper articles and discussions that include so many different descriptions of Dancehall, they would make anyone's head spin. The definitions vary depending on whether you are a young newly exposed Jamaican music enthusiast, or a foreigner in some far away country. Our inability to accurately define this very vibrant aspect of Jamaican culture is another example of what happens when we fail to treat local music and entertainment as a structured business. Unfortunately, we may very well have to contend with this dilemma of informality for quite some time, as it appears that some of the biggest promoters of Dancehall music are of the view that Dancehall by nature can only thrive in an unstructured environment. I however beg to differ on that point.

As far as I am aware, the term Dance Hall was first used to describe the venue where dances were kept in Jamaica several decades ago. It is also my understanding that over time this definition has evolved to become the description of a new music genre derived from Reggae around the mid-1980s. I spent 12 years of my music business career managing and working very closely with producers Steely and Clevie who are recognized as the pioneers in the production of the rhythms that characterized Dancehall as a music genre. I therefore subscribe to the definition of Dancehall as a new genre derived from Reggae. There is ongoing debate however between many of our established musicians as to whether there is in fact a difference between Reggae and Dancehall as music genres. Some say Reggae and Dancehall are one and the same, while others argue that they are different music genres, in very much the same way that Ska is different from Mento. Today Dancehall is also used as a term

---

58. http://www.jamaicaobserver.com/latestnews/Abrupt-end-for-Sting-2014
59. https://www.facebook.com/notes/lloyd-stanbury/what-is-dancehall/10150150701970355

to describe the lifestyle that is identified with this new "branch" of Reggae, hence we have Dancehall culture.

Jamaica has had a very rich tradition in popular music that has gained the attention of persons all over the world. Over the past 60 years our music has evolved, primarily through African, Rastafarian and North American influences, to create recognizable genres such as Mento, Ska, Rock Steady, Reggae and now Dancehall. Despite this, we have failed to take the lead in clearly defining our music forms, resulting in today's confusion about what is Dancehall. I even read where someone described all Jamaican music created over the past 60 years as Dancehall music.

Our failure to clearly and consistently define and present to the wider global audience what we have created musically, has allowed others to categorize us as they see fit. I have very vivid memories of an attempt a few years ago by the Grammy committee to remove Sean Paul from the Reggae Grammy category and place him in the Rap category. This move was however stopped through a petition signed by several persons actively involved in the Reggae music business. Our failure to define what we have created in Dancehall has also allowed other top international artists such as R Kelly, Rihanna, Beyonce and others to perform our musical genre and call it pop and/or R&B. As someone said in one of those articles I mentioned earlier, Jamaicans need to wake up and smell the Blue Mountain Coffee.

From Sting to Rebel Salute
- Facebook note, December 29, 2014 [60]

The 31st annual staging of the Sting one night festival has come and gone, and as is typical, left most supporters of Jamaican music and culture gasping for breath. Personally "I can't breathe" from the Stink. For too long this event has been allowed to promote lyrical clashes and uncontrolled verbal abuse on stage as a representation of Jamaican entertainment. We are also in really deep shit when our Minister of Culture Lisa Hanna sees it fit to publicly proclaim

---

60. https://www.facebook.com/notes/lloyd-stanbury/from-sting-to-rebel-salute/10155517489720355?pnref=lhc

her support for an event that gives priority to vulgarity and violence, rather than the presentation of musical performances.[61]

Give thanks for the courage and vision of Tony Rebel, who has for over 20 years presented the Rebel Salute festival, and stuck to his goal of showcasing real Jamaican music that exemplifies healthy lifestyles and celebrate the cultural impact and significance of Rastafari.

The lines are clearly drawn, and solutions to the dilemma facing Jamaica in our quest for sustainable development rest squarely on our abilities to appreciate the significance of culture, and our cultural industries. Even Former Prime Minister PJ Patterson, who wasted his opportunity to make a difference during his tenure in office, seems to now see the light. His recent utterances about the value of marijuana and Jamaican music are actually quite interesting. [62]

There seems to be a vast gap between the thinking of former Prime Minister Patterson, and the views of the young Culture Minister, who many once saw as our future leader. Maybe Minister Hanna needs to move from Sting to Rebel Salute.

Summary

- There is a great deal of controversy and misunderstanding about the differences between Dance Hall the space and Dancehall the music genre.
- Some musicians regard Dancehall as just another form of Reggae, while others see it as a separate genre or sub-genre.
- Dancehall music has been stigmatized as promoting materialism, violence and sex.
- Many regard the emergence and popularity of dancehall music as a deliberate strategy to silence and sideline more politically progressive and militant Reggae music.
- Creative musical elements of dancehall music have been widely embraced by non-Jamaican musicians including Spanish-speaking musicians from Latin America and the Caribbean in the creation of what is now called Reggaeton.

---

61. http://vimeopro.com/ymytv/videos/video/80434153
62. http://www.jamaicaobserver.com/news/-Ganja--Green-Gold-

Copeland Forbes is the most experienced Jamaican artist manager and tour manager in Reggae. © 2015 Sista Irie Photography

Reggae music's most successful entrepreneur **Chris Blackwell** with **Rita Marley**, Minister of Culture **Babsy Grange**, and **Grace Jones**, at the Reggae Academy Awards 2008 in Kingston. © 2008 Lance Watson Photography

Rastafari elder, Nyabinghi drummer and chanter Prof I reasoning with Lloyd Stanbury in Ocho Rios, Jamaica. © 2015 Sista Irie Photography

Ras Michael of Ras Michael and the Sons of Negus. A pioneer in the commercial recording and performance of Nyabinghi music. © 2013 Sista Irie Photography

Jimmy Cliff, through his very successful movie "The Harder They Come" with soundtrack recoding of the same name, became one of the first Jamaican artists to gain popularity in Africa and other countries around the world. © 2015 Sista Irie Photography

Linton "Kwesi" Johnson, a Jamaican UK based poet, was one of the first recording artists from Jamaica to create an impact within the Caribbean communities of England with his politically charged poetry put to Reggae music in the early 1970s. © 2014 Sista Irie Photography

Ivorian Reggae singer **Alpha Blondy** rose to international prominence as a leading Reggae artist from Africa with his first solo album released in 1982. © 2013 Sista Irie Photography

David Hinds, lead vocalist, guitarist and songwriter from the legendary band Steel Pulse, one of the first Reggae bands to make it big within the Caribbean communities of England. © 2012 Sista Irie Photography

Tabernacle at Pinnacle, the first self sufficient Rastafari community established in the hills of St. Catherine Jamaica by Leonard Percival Howell. © 2014 Sista Irie Photography

Israel Vibration was one of the early Reggae successes coming out of the Twelve Tribes of Israel Rastafari Mansion. Their debut single "Why Worry" was released on the Twelve Tribes record label in 1976. © 2012 Sista Irie Photography

Capleton is one of the first Rasta Reggae artists of the Bobo Ashanti mansion to receive international recognition and acclaim when he was signed to Def Jam Recordings in the USA. © 2015 Sista Irie Photography

Big Youth came to prominence in the early 1970s as one of the first popular Rasta DJ/Chanters from Jamaica, and was signed to Virgin Records' Frontline label. © 2015 Sista Irie Photography

The Rebel Salute annual music festival has survived and grown throughout the period of dancehall music dominance in Jamaica, although it emphasizes traditional roots Reggae music. © 2015 Sista Irie Photography

U Roy is widely recognized as a pioneer of the phenomenon of toasting in Reggae music, which heralded the birth of American Hip-Hop music and the vocal styling now commonly used by dancehall Deejays. © 2015 Sista Irie Photography

Dancehall recording artist **Busy Signal** has been a regular participant in recent stagings of the annual roots Reggae festival Rebel Salute. © 2014 Sista Irie Photography

Agent Sasco aka Assassin has represented the dancehall music genre with significant levels of success both locally and internationally. He has also been a spokesman for professionalism in the music industry. © 2008 Lance Watson Photography

Dons, Gangsters, and Illegal Drugs

Criminal activities, ranging from the illicit drug trade to gun violence, have unfortunately been associated with the production and presentation of Reggae for many years. Several well-known artists, music producers and show promoters from Jamaica have been implicated in ongoing political gang warfare. The list of Jamaican artists and music producers accused and/or convicted of violent and non-violent criminal activity is a long one. It seems reasonable to assume that these factors can negatively affect global positioning of a production. However, as we have noted, there is a sub-culture that provides a market segment for that type of artist and lyric, not only from within the genre of Reggae.

Politics, Garrison Communities and Drug Trafficking

In Chapter 4, under the section "Socio-Political Considerations Regarding Reggae and Dancehall", mention is made of the impact of political violence on Jamaican communities, and the connection with music. Many reports have suggested that community leaders and enforcers were initially created in Jamaica through the influence of politicians in their efforts to gain support to secure votes to win elections. As a result of this relationship between community leaders and political parties, a number of communities have been established with almost one hundred percent allegiance to one or the other of two leading political parties in Jamaica, the JLP, or the PNP. These communities are commonly referred to as "garrisons". Tivoli Gardens (JLP) and Arnett Gardens (PNP) are two of the most well-known "garrison" communities in Jamaica.

Within every 'garrison' there are community leaders, referred to as "Dons", who are typically strong-arm men and gang leaders with an army of enforcers. Traditionally 'garrison Dons' secure their support from favours and contracts awarded by the government and politicians they support, but over time most 'garrison' leaders have branched off into other activities such as drug trafficking, dealing in arms, and the production and promotion of music.

Illegal drug trafficking and dealing in arms have become an entrenched feature of Jamaican 'garrison' communities. These activities have also provided a level of independence for the community leaders from the influence and control of the local politician. This phenomenon is exemplified by the internationally publicized case of Christopher "Dudus" Coke, the alleged leader of the notorious "Shower Posse" gang affiliated with Tivoli Gardens and the Jamaica Labour Party. Coke was extradited to the USA in 2010.[63]

The upfront participation of PNP government ministers Omar Davis, Peter Phillips, and Karl Blythe at the funeral of murdered garrison Don, William "Willie Haggart" Moore, was cited as an example of the close connection between politicians and gangsters in Jamaica.[64] Both "Dudus" and "Willie Haggart" were very closely linked with recording artists and the promotion of music events in Garrison communities.

Garrisons, Dons and Music

A large percentage of Jamaican Reggae and Dancehall artists have emerged from the inner city communities of Jamaica where Dons and Garrison life are almost inescapable. The allure of the business of music as a source for money laundering, and the desire of emerging artists to gain access, street credibility and acceptance in Garrison communities, provided fertile ground for the establishment of music business relationships and opportunities for local and internationally based Dons.

Many Reggae and Dancehall concerts in Jamaica, the USA, the UK and Canada have been financed by Dons, and several well-known show

---

63. http://abcnews.go.com/Blotter/jamaican-drug-lord-christopher-dudus-coke-23-years/story?id=16527584

64. http://www.telegraph.co.uk/news/worldnews/centralamericaandthecaribbean/jamaica/1333981/Through-drugs-and-ingenuity-the-dons-are-now-independent-of-politicians.html

promotion companies have been established and are closely associated with Dons. There have also been recording studios built and record labels formed that have been closely associated with Dons and other persons alleged to be involved in illegal drug trafficking. The connection between drug trafficking money, and the production and promotion of Reggae and Dancehall has been such, that it is often argued that gangsters and illegal drugs have provided the greatest source of financing for the Reggae/Dancehall business inside Jamaica.

The implications of the close relationship between Jamaican music and the underworld of illegal drugs, gangs, and violent crime have been far reaching. The significance of the interconnection is also clearly demonstrated in the popularity of music and artists that lyrically address the issues of gangs, crime and violence. The very popular and controversial recording *Look Into My Eyes* by Dancehall artist Bounty Killa provides a perfect example.[65]

Several well-known Jamaican recording artists, music producers, show promoters, sound system operators and selectors, have been implicated or convicted of criminal activities. The debate continues on whether Reggae/Dancehall music lyrics describing crime and violence are merely a reflection of the societal realities, or on the other hand, contribute to the ongoing problem of crime and violence in Jamaica. It is however quite clear that the international image of Reggae and Dancehall has suffered from the association of some Jamaican artists and events with crime and violence. This is also reflected in the increased incidence of travel visa and work permit denials to Jamaican artists seeking admission to the USA, UK, Canada and neighbouring Caribbean countries. Some live venues and promoters in the USA, UK and Canada have also shown reduced interest in doing business with Jamaican artists due to real or perceived association with crime and criminal activities.

The Impact of Illegal Drugs and Drug Abuse

The association of illegal drug trafficking with the financing of music production and promotion activities is not unique to Jamaica. In his 2008 book "Sounding Salsa", Columbia University professor Christopher Washburne devotes an entire chapter to the story of how the increased popularity of cocaine in the early 1970s coincided with the explosion of

---

65. https://www.youtube.com/watch?v=krheYTjREsQ

musical creativity by a label and a group of musicians that changed the sound of Latin music. Washburne wrote that individuals associated with Colombian-based cartels infiltrated every level of the music industry as they became "key partners in the music's production and distribution." In Jamaica the existence of Dons within the politically charged and partisan garrison communities was largely supported by money secured from illegal drug trafficking.

Jamaica's emergence as a trans-shipment point for South American cocaine on its way to North America has had a significant impact on the local music industry. At the turn of the century a U.S. State Department report listed Jamaica as the leading trans-shipment port in the Caribbean region for cocaine destined for the U.S.A. Not only did Jamaica become a trans-shipment point, but cocaine use also escalated on the island. The access to cocaine inside Jamaica increased significantly between the 1970s and the end of the century, resulting in many artists being exposed to and becoming cocaine users. The close connection between drug traffickers from Jamaican garrison communities and individuals in the music industry resulted in many partnerships to produce and promote music. In many instances trading in illegal drugs was seen as a precursor to establishing a music business enterprise.

The intermingling of illegal drug trafficking and drug use with the activities of Jamaican music industry practitioners has had negative repercussions in a number of cases, many of which have not been publicized. The lure of illegal drug trafficking has been the focus of much controversy in the well-publicized Buju Banton cocaine case. [66]

Music, Crime and Violence
– Facebook note, May 16, 2010 [67]

Who feels it, knows it. I quote this phrase today in reference to the scourge of crime and gun violence that has now invaded and taken control of the lives of many young Jamaicans. My comments are made not only as an active participant in the Jamaican music industry, but also as someone who has experienced first-hand the

---

66. http://www.dailymail.co.uk/news/article-2007387/Buju-Banton-Grammy-winning-Reggae-star-jailed-10-years-cocaine-deal.html

67. https://www.facebook.com/notes/lloyd-stanbury/music-crime-and-violence/10150191618025355

negative effects of gun violence, and a firm advocate against negative Dancehall lyrics that glorify crime.

The recent shootings of top Dancehall artists Mad Cobra and O'Neil Edwards of Voice Mail have resulted in renewed calls for Jamaican artists and the nation as a whole to take a stand against the crime and violence that has overtaken the Island. It is definitely now time for all well thinking Jamaicans and fans of Reggae and Dancehall to withdraw their support from artists and music producers who continue to produce and promote songs with lyrics that glorify guns, violence and gangsters. In my opinion there is no place in today's Jamaica for songwriters, performers and music producers who dedicate time and resources to making and promoting such songs, and who tell their fans that "Informer fi dead".

I am not by any means suggesting that the Dancehall artists alone are responsible for the upsurge in crime and violence in recent years. The reality is that there are many and varied reasons for the apparent lack of respect for human life among Jamaicans, and our inability to resolve issues without resort to violence. I do however subscribe to the view that recording artists have had a significant negative impact on the values and attitudes of our young people, and that a reversal of these negatives will require some positive input from persons in the music industry. Many artists contend that their musical works are merely a reflection of what they observe in the society. I do agree that some lyrics are written with that objective. It is however also abundantly clear to me that many artists have lost their way by trying to live and portray a lifestyle that is in keeping with the crime and violence reflected in their lyrics.

Now that the guns that have been the subject of glorification in music have been turned on artists within the Dancehall community, the reactions so far are indeed quite interesting, and in some cases very hypocritical. Some persons who have now decided to speak out against negative Dancehall lyrics were either silent or defenders of this kind of music not too long ago while they were beneficiaries of the income generated from it.

No one, whether he or she is an artist, a 5 year old child, or just a regular law- abiding citizen, deserves to be shot by a common criminal. As a participant in the local music fraternity, I join in condemning the brutal acts of violence against our colleagues. I would also however like to urge performers, music producers, promoters and media representatives to act now and do their part to bring about a change in our attitudes towards each other by making and supporting more positive music. We need to support music that encourages love and unity. We need to support music that brings more attention to the corruption, injustices and discrimination that now seem to be an accepted part of life in Jamaica.

Criminality and the Jamaican Music Industry
– Facebook note, October 1, 2011[68]

In the recent past we have seen more news locally and internationally about the alleged criminal activities of Jamaican artists than we have had news of their international chart topping or concert tour successes. The list of Jamaican artists who have been accused, arrested or convicted of crimes over the past five years is frightening, and should be cause for concern from supporters of Jamaican music as well as anyone seeking to pursue a career in the Jamaican entertainment industry.

It is a sad reality that in Jamaica today there appears to be no distinction between criminality on the one hand, and the pursuit of genuine professional activities within the Jamaican music industry on the other. The line between criminality and entertainment in Jamaica is so blurred that many media practitioners and "so called" entertainment industry experts assume that the role of an entertainment lawyer is to defend entertainers who get involved in criminal activities. I have been practicing entertainment law for over 30 years, which means I specialize in providing legal advice and guidance on contracts and intellectual property law issues to artists, producers, managers, promoters and others involved in music, film and media. In the recent past however I have been bombarded with more inquiries and comments in relation to my opinion on criminal matters concerning Jamaican entertainers than I have been asked to provide services for entertainment contracts or copyright issues.

There will be many explanations offered as reasons for the

---

68. https://www.facebook.com/notes/lloyd-stanbury/criminality-and-the-jamaican-music-industry/10150844319525355

upsurge in reports on the alleged criminal activities of Jamaican artists. I would however like to take the position of offering some solutions. I believe we, (government, private sector investors, and industry practitioners) need to focus more of our attention on the following:

1. The decriminalization of Marijuana in Jamaica.
2. The provision of development capital/funding for music industry projects in an effort to reduce the dependence of local music industry practitioners on funding from drug traffickers and gun runners.
3. The recognition of the need for training in entertainment management, and the provision of adequate facilities for such training.
4. The development of and support for relevant music industry organizations to facilitate more order and the establishment of standards for the local music industry.

There needs to be a concerted effort to separate criminality from the business of music in Jamaica. We cannot afford to continue paying lip-service to the development of our creative industries and the preservation of our cultural assets. As the majority of well-thinking Jamaicans and friends of Jamaica now call for an end to government corruption and garrison politics, so too should we insist on measures to protect one of our most valuable assets, our music.

Summary

- Criminal activity has been associated with certain aspects of Jamaican music for a long time.
- In some Jamaican communities political gangs have closely aligned themselves with the business of music.
- Artists have come under more scrutiny by immigration authorities worldwide due to the perception of criminality associated with Jamaican music.
- Money from illegal drug trafficking has provided funding for many Jamaican music business operations.
- There are divergent opinions as to whether music with violent lyrics

promotes crime or just reflects the ills of society.

- Ganja is used and promoted by many Jamaican artists, and the criminalization of ganja has adversely affected the careers of many artists.

Women and Reggae

2007 survey conducted by the Women's Resource and Outreach Centre in Jamaica revealed that well over 50 percent of the Jamaican population is female, and that women are graduating from universities in Jamaica at a four-to-one ratio. Despite these statistics, the survey also showed that women made up fewer than 10 percent of law makers in the House of Representatives in Jamaica, and accounted for only 16 percent of the Board of Directors of private companies and 33 percent of public sector organizations.[69]

One explanation given for the imbalance revealed by the study is the persistence of a closed circle of influence dominated by men, and fueled by the erroneous perception of the role of women in society. In recent years this situation has changed for the better, as the Jamaican society becomes more mature with the recognition that women do have a lot to say and contribute to development.

The efforts of Jamaican diplomat, author, and gender specialist Lucille Mathurin-Mair have gone a long way in creating an enlightened approach to the role of women in the Jamaican society. Her book "The Rebel Woman in the British West Indies During Slavery" has been an inspiration for many and is often referenced in programs of the Institute of Gender Studies at the University of the West Indies (UWI) Mona, Jamaica. The UWI's Caribbean Institute of Women in Leadership

---

69. http://jamaica-gleaner.com/gleaner/20110915/lead/lead3.html

(CIWIL), and the Women's Resource and Outreach Centre in Jamaica have come together to undertake several initiatives aimed at correcting the imbalance regarding the involvement of women in various aspects of Jamaican economic, political and social life. Their plan is to create, through training and support programs, an environment where more women can seek out and occupy positions of leadership.

The level of female participation in Jamaican leadership positions and in business is also reflected in the Reggae music community. Women in Reggae have also faced additional barriers and challenges that are emphasized by certain practices that have become common in the Jamaican music industry. The percentage of Jamaican women who actively participate and succeed in Reggae as artists, artist representatives, and providers of support services is very low, and may even be lower than other areas of economic, social and political activity. The tendency of some artists and others in the music industry to promote lyrical content and live music performances that project negative images of women compounds the problem.

In the face of this low level of representation of women in Reggae locally, it is somewhat ironic that the Jamaican artists who received the most international mainstream media attention in 2013 and 2014 were both women. In 2013 Jamaica's Tessanne Chin came out winner of Season 5 of the American TV show "The Voice", the most watched programme on television in the USA, and televised globally by NBC. In 2014 Jamaican Reggae singer Anita Antoinette made it to the top 10 of Season 7 of "The Voice" and received rave reviews and major mainstream exposure.

Female Artists in Reggae

When compared with other music genres, Jamaican popular music has a very low percentage of women who are visibly active, and who attain success as solo performers, lead vocalists of bands, songwriters and music producers. In the 1960s and 1970s the level of female activity in Jamaican music, though low, was higher than the later years of the 1980s, 1990s and early 2000s. Artists such as Millie Small, Hortense Ellis, Cynthia Richards, Marcia Griffiths, Judy Mowatt, Lorna Bennett, Sharon Forrester, Susan Cadogan, Cynthia Schloss, Dawn Penn, Phyllis Dillon, Pam Hall, Sheila Hylton, and Rita Marley held their own both locally and internationally with hit recordings and frequent concert appearances.

In the late 1980s, through to the 1990s and 2000s, the popularity of the Dancehall sub-genre of Reggae brought with it a greater degree of male domination. Most of the popular Dancehall recordings and events in Jamaica have been characterized as somewhat hardcore, with a combination of violent and sexually aggressive lyrics. Much of the lyrics in Dancehall is also seen as degrading and disrespectful to women. This may have contributed to a decline in the number of female artists actively involved in recording and performing in Jamaica in the years that Dancehall music reigned. In recent years (since 2009), the resurgence in Jamaica of traditional roots Reggae has opened the doors for female artists such as Queen Ifrica, Etana, Jah9, Kelissa, Alaine, Hempress Sativa, and more pop-Reggae oriented artists such as Tessanne Chin.

Traditionally female artists in Jamaica have been relegated to the roles of live back-up vocalists and studio harmony singers. The talents of women as vocal arrangers, songwriters, music producers and lead vocalists have been somewhat stifled, leading to deficiencies in the variety of production and presentation in Jamaican music. Many women who have performed behind-the-scenes creative roles, have been deprived of the credits and the resulting royalties that flow from the commercial exploitation of original musical compositions and sound recordings to which they contribute.

The imbalance in the number of women involved as artists in the Jamaican music industry has contributed to less than adequate levels of growth and industry development. Having worked in various capacities in the Jamaican music and entertainment industry, it is my observation that a much larger number of creative and talented women exists than is represented by the percentage of successful female artists compared to men. There needs to be an analysis of the circumstances in which women operate in music in Jamaica, and remedial measures taken to lessen the barriers and challenges they face.

Women in the Business of Reggae

Unlike their creative counterparts, women are fairly well represented in the business aspects of Reggae music. The leading Reggae music distribution company in the world, VP Records, is headed by Patricia Chin. She is the P in VP, which was started by herself and her now deceased husband Vincent in 1979. In the formative years of Jamaican popular music, Sonia Pottinger played a major role as music producer and record label executive. She is responsible for numerous hit recordings from the 1960s and 1970s that were released on her Gay Feet, Tip Top, Rainbow and High Note record labels. Bob Andy, Marcia Griffiths, Culture, U-Roy and Big Youth are some of the artists with albums produced by Sonia Pottinger.

Jamaican women have also figured prominently in the area of artist management. Member of Parliament and former Minister of Culture Olivia "Babsy" Grange was one of the first successful Jamaican artist managers operating internationally. In the 1970s she represented Leroy Sibblies and Carlene Davis while they were residing in Canada, and later partnered with Clifton "Specialist" Dillon to form the SPECS-SHANG company that managed Shabba Ranks, Mad Cobra, Lady Patra, Richie Stephens, and Bounti Killa. Several women have launched and maintained successful careers and businesses as artist managers, booking agents, and publicists providing services to prominent Reggae stars inside and outside Jamaica. There may even be more successful female artists managers, booking agents and publicists in Reggae than there are men.

Opinions of Women in Reggae

It would be unfair and disrespectful to speak of women involved in Reggae and not have them address the issues in their own voice as they see them. Here are some opinions of a selection of artists, technicians and media practitioners with many years' experience in the industry.

Tanya Stephens – Songwriter and Recording Artist

Over the years my interpretation of 'female barriers' has gone through a few changes. After my pregnancy I experienced the ostracism which the un-established female faces during and after pregnancy. With the benefit of maturity I realized the lyrical content of my material had a big part to play. At that time I mostly sang about male-female relationships, using sexual encounters to bring my points across. It would have been pretty awkward and tasteless having a pregnant woman on stage talking about bad sex. My decision to be a mother after birth of my child, including accepting the responsibility of bonding and breastfeeding, gave me a different perspective and approach.

After many years of experience and objective observation, I have concluded that the biggest challenge women in the industry face is their individual and collective attitude toward the business of music. Most women I encounter seem to have a sense of entitlement, and think they deserve a spot at the top by virtue of everything except a hit song or audience approval. This is fed mostly by the media, and no amount of audience rejection affects that resolve.

I do not think underrepresentation of women in Reggae has affected the advancement of the industry. People listen to music, not genitalia. I think we have suffered setbacks because of the increasing absence of talented musicians in the studio. Our music has become less musical.

I do not think any imbalance in society has created an imbalance in the music industry's male/female ratio. All the men who aspire to become artists are firmly rooted in the thought that they have to work very hard. Not all are equally talented, but they share a similar drive. The females on the other hand have been socialized to compete aesthetically and through shock value, rather than be creatively substantive, hence their low numbers.

Tandra Lytes Jhagroo – Audio Engineer

I can't say that I have faced too many barriers, I'm not inhibited by the technology and I keep up to date with it. Is there an invisible boys club? Sort of. Am I cool enough to be in it? Yes and no. Does it affect me? Not one bit. As you grow in and around the music business, you find all sorts of areas to get into, and that's how I chose to interact.

In my opinion women are under-represented behind the mic, but in front the mic it's a matter of those who succeed, versus those who can't.

I think a lot of female acts come and go. Do they stick? Not really. I sometimes wonder why. Is it because of the bottleneck effect in the studio where all the boys know the technology and the girls don't really pick up so readily? Very few girls make it to producer status, but there are a lot of female managers, booking agents and publicists that are doing well.

Creating music is a tough process. Luckily Jamaica is a place where you can try and try again, but for some reason it seems women stop trying after a while. I do wish that they would keep trying, and I always encourage them to, where I can, both in the studio and while I was teaching.

I don't think that most women will be honest about the challenges they face in Reggae, mainly because of the sensitivity of some issues, and for fear of being labeled or being the subject of further discrimination.

Sista Irie – Radio Dj and Photojournalist

Working primarily as a Reggae radio host and photojournalist I have not had many challenges. That said, I think the absence of issues in my case, is the result of a commitment from the very beginning to always conduct myself with professionalism. Since most Reggae artists are men, it was important to choose between wanting/having personal relationships with the artists, or staying committed to my interactions with them as work. Over time, the respect is now well established.

If there are challenges, it is because some artists, as much as they may want media support, will often cancel or get distracted when young women fans are available. If I were to give advice to the artists, I would say make sure your professional life comes first and don't underestimate the value of a good relationship with members of the press.

I think it is a shame women are not given equal respect and recognition in the Reggae music industry, but I don't know that I could say it has held the business back as much as other factors. Women in the industry certainly balance out the vibes and establish a deeper sense of female power which has been missing. Reggae music has demonstrated that duets of male and female artists are for the most part successful. More female backup singers need to be given adequate solo time on stage.

For the most part, Jamaica has the appearance of a patriarchal society. Too many women are abused, neglected and mistreated, so it is not surprising they are not given equality in the music industry. It is also a shame that women are many times portrayed as sex objects leading to young girls buying into it and undervaluing their own potentials.

Pam Hall – Songwriter, Producer and Recording Artist

I see the challenges faced by female artists as developmental and also as a microcosm of the wider world, where women are coming from a long way back. Consider the times when women could neither own property nor vote. Problems such as sexual harassment apply not just to music but the wider society. The challenges that I personally have had to face are professional ones such as effective promotion (that is the big one faced by all artists), production expenses and simply being able to improve one's knowledge base in order to achieve maximum effectiveness in the business.

I don't think the business of Reggae has suffered any particular setback because of the paucity of female artists, as this situation has been rapidly changing with not only many more female artists but also managers, producers, lawyers, agents, etc. If it had continued as it started, with only a handful of female artists, then that would have definitely been a drawback. The increased availability of technological tools such as computers, internet and social media, as well as the broadening of the support personnel in the industry is making it easier for more female artists to enter the industry.

I think the imbalance in numbers is basically a reflection of the Jamaican society as a whole. The music business, however, is a hard row to hoe, and traditionally would not be the average family's choice of career for their female members. There is also a bias in favour of male artists. As women move upward in society as a whole, however, we see this situation changing, although I do not foresee equal numbers of male versus female artists at any time to come, and I don't think equal numbers is a necessity. A fair numerical representation of female artists, and equitable and just treatment of all artists is more important than equal numbers.

DJ Sparks – Radio DJ and Publicist

When I first wanted to learn how to mix to become a DJ the men were generally reluctant to teach me. I finally got some good teachers. I saved up and got myself a DJ console and practiced my heart out.

There are male DJs who operate in cliques, who would tell promoters not to book you. Many promoters are unsure of the capabilities of female DJs, mainly because they are unaccustomed to seeing a woman in this role. In addition to being female, I am of a lighter skin colour, I wear glasses, and completed university. In the domain of Dancehall, I do not fit the stereotype of a DJ. I therefore recognized my role in the game as cutting a path for future generations of female DJs, so that we are not seen as an anomaly.

The music field is male dominated in Jamaica, which is a patriar-

chal society. Males are therefore territorial. They like women as long as they know their place. For the most part my career has been about knocking down barriers and climbing the mountain so that people see my talent. What doesn't kill you makes you stronger

I have no empirical evidence to support the statement that the advancement of the business of Reggae has suffered setbacks because of the under representation of women in the industry. It may bear some truth but I am not sure to what extent.

Some women play like males but that might be due to them trying to emulate the men because that is all they see, and because the public has been trained by the males on how to receive the music.

Etana – Songwriter and Recording Artist

The main challenge I've had is to be seen just as an artist, and not a female artist who is considered less than a male. I always have to prove myself, because of the belief that females can't pull the crowd like a man can, and I often get paid less than my male counterparts.

I have had challenges with being able to travel with my band all the time, and am often asked to work with the backing band of male artists on the same show. Even though I have proven myself in many of these cases, it seems never ending, as the next day in another territory I have to prove myself again, but they always come around. After proving myself I can do what I want – LOL

I don't think the under-representation of women in Reggae has caused a setback. My reason for saying this is I have heard this over and over again "Do you know a certain person in Jamaica who can get my money back from so and so? They got money from us and never showed up". Or "they sang for half the time they were booked for and threw the microphone down, cursed and walked off". I can go on and on.

I also believe that if most of the people in the Reggae industry were not so stuck in their selfish ways, we could be much further ahead, but the info known by most of the successful people who have been in it for a while, is stuck somewhere deep inside them. Also the mistakes that others made in the past were never addressed or corrected so the younger ones have to come and face it.

I am in total agreement that the imbalance in the number of women in Reggae versus men is a mere reflection of the imbalances in other as-

pects of Jamaican society. It's not just a Jamaican thing. I's a Caribbean thing. It's an African thing, it's a chauvinistic thing, where men are taught that a woman's place is in the kitchen, and every woman "affi get @#%*" LOL. I laugh, but a couple of times I had to make it known that I am not the girl next door that you know, or that friends know about, so straighten up. I am Etana and I treat you with respect, and it must be reciprocated. I have been called many names for my mannerism and stance, like bitch and miserable, but if you simply smile for everything then the seriousness goes away for everyone and they all feel they can either disrespect you easily, or put in a word or two to see how easy it would be to get in my underwear. I do believe it is changing a little bit though, where women are more respected on show posters, are being made headliners, and are having their time on stage respected. I have spoken to a few artists before me, such as Lady Saw, Lady G, Marcia Griffiths, Tanya Stephens, and they all agree women have to work twice or three times as hard.

I would advise young women seeking to enter the Reggae business to get to know as much about the business as possible, but don't allow the business to get in the way of your creativity. Stay focused and don't become overly aggressive to the point where you lose sight of your goals, or who or what is important at the moment to get to the next step. Follow your plan as much as possible, but remember to follow your heart. You have to really love it, and if it is about the money first, you will give up quickly. Say what you mean and keep your legs closed unless its your heart's desire, and never for status or material gain. It will fade pretty quickly. Straight face, wise mind and heart.

Women in Reggae
– Facebook note, August 27, 2014 [70]

Isn't it ironic that the two Jamaican artists that have received the most international promotion and exposure in 2013 and 2014 are female, while inside Jamaica women continue to struggle in the male dominated Reggae and Dancehall music space?

In the early days of Jamaican popular music, female singers and songwriters played a major role in taking the music onto the world stage. One of the first major international Jamaican hit re-

---

70. https://www.facebook.com/notes/lloyd-stanbury/women-in-Reggae/10155058416390355

cordings was by Millie Small, with her early 1960s million-selling single "My Boy Lollipop." Its success opened the doors for such artists as Phyllis Dillon, Marcia Griffiths, Judy Mowatt, Hortense Ellis, Pam Hall, Rita Marley, Carlene Davis, J.C. Lodge, Cynthia Schloss, Lorna Bennett, Sharon Forrester, Dawn Penn, Sheila Hylton, Susan Cadogan and Nadine Sutherland, all of whom established themselves as mainstream recording and performing artists in the 1970s and 1980s.

For some strange reason, however, the early successes of these female artists did not result in the kind of follow-through accomplished by their male counterparts. It is my opinion that over the past two decades, women have not been adequately represented as artists in Jamaican music business. With the exception of the local and international successes of Diana King, Patra, Sasha, Foxy Brown, Tanya Stephens, and Lady Saw, female Reggae and Dancehall stars became a very scarce commodity.

The low level of female representation in Reggae is in my view a barrier to the advancement of the industry. A number of reasons have been put   forward to explain the problem. Sexual harassment by music producers, artist managers, and other male industry participants, and the rough and aggressive nature of male-dominated Dancehall music are two examples. The tendency of many young Jamaican female artists to idolize and follow foreign Pop and R&B female stars is another argument put forward for the low number of successful Jamaican female Reggae stars in recent decades. Maybe our female Reggae pioneers should be embraced more as role models.

In recent years however, we have witnessed the emergence of a number of very talented and successful female artists in Reggae and Dancehall. This new influx of women in Reggae is a welcome sign and one to be encouraged. The Dancehall success of artists such as Ce'Cile has influenced many women who might previously have had a hard time because of their social background. Tanya Stephens has also helped pave the way with her accomplishments as a very talented songwriter and recording artist.

Today's "Women in Reggae" seem to be doing better at holding their own as artists in the very challenging global music market, and some may even have positioned themselves to take the lead in charting the course for the future of Reggae music on the international scene. Artists such as Tessanne, Anita Antoinette, Jah9, Kelissa, Semantha J, Alaine, Tami Chynn, Etana, Spice, Jovi Rockwell, Cherine Anderson, Queen Ifrica, Kris Kelly, and Brick and Lace have clearly signaled the long-awaited return of female Reggae recording artists and performers. Whatever the reason for this recent upsurge in female talent, we should be thankful and do everything possible to encourage and support the trend.

Radio, club and sound system DJs, as well as show promoters, now need to display more respect for the role and contribution of women to our music, and to the development of the industry, by featuring more female recording artists in their programs and live events. With the aggression and heartlessness now rampant in our communities, we do need an injection of the softer, kinder, more loving messages that music can provide, and who better to do this than our strong, caring Reggae women. The women in Reggae have not only demonstrated their ability to record and perform at the highest level, they have also shown that they can speak intelligently and properly represent Reggae, and Jamaica, as was clearly demonstrated by both Tessanne and Anita Antoinette in their appearances on "The Voice"

There could never be a better time for the return of the ladies in Reggae. Let's hope that we will see and hear more of them in future.

Summary

- Women are under-represented in the creative aspects of the Jamaican music industry.
- A greater percentage of women operate successfully in the business and management side of the Jamaican music industry than on the creative side.

Reggae, Globalization & Technology

The movement, interdependence and interconnectivity of information and human capital facilitated by rapid technological changes,
have had a profound impact on the way we produce and consume
entertainment and cultural products and services in the 21st century. The
phenomenon of globalization has resulted in the music industry becoming
more homogenized in terms of genre distinctions, and new technologies
have given rise to music business models that were unheard of a mere
ten years ago. The maker and marketer of music must be familiar with
the technologies, their reach and their language if they are to have any
measure of success in the globalized, digital age.

Migration and Globalization

Globalization is defined as a process of international integration
as a result of the exchange of ideas, world views, products, and culture
between nations and regions. Transportation and communication are
major factors in globalization, and technological advances made in these
areas, including the emergence of the Internet, have generated greater
interdependence in economic and cultural activities. In recent decades
(since the 1980s), there has been a noticeable increase in the use of the
term globalization. In 2000 the International Monetary Fund (IMF)
outlined four basic aspects of globalization to include: trade and transac-
tions, capital and investment movements, migration and movement of
people, and the dissemination of knowledge.

112

From a Jamaican perspective migration and the effects of globalization on culture and trade could be examined against the background of activities that occurred over the past 500 years. Jamaican lifestyle, economic activities and culture have been significantly impacted by the arrival in the Caribbean of European explorers between the end of the 15th century and the middle of the 17th century. Jamaica was first colonized by the Spanish at the beginning of the 16th century, and then by the British, in the mid-17th century. Spanish and British rule have influenced and shaped philosophy, religion, language, the arts, and other aspects of Jamaican culture as a result of the exchange of ideas and economic activities that occurred.

The invasion and colonization of Jamaica by Spanish and British explorers included the forced importation of Africans as slaves. It is estimated that between the years 1500 and 1800 approximately eleven million African slaves were brought to the Caribbean. Most of the slaves taken to Jamaica were from West, Central and East African regions. Subsequent to the abolition of slavery in Jamaica in 1833, the British colonizers engaged in the importation of indentured workers, primarily from India, as well as from China.

Jamaica's migration experiences also include the outward movement of people to other countries. Historically, Jamaican emigration has been at a relatively high level. Movement out of Jamaica started from the late 1800 into the early 1900s when many Jamaicans migrated to Cuba, the Dominican Republic, and Central America to work on the Panama Canal and on banana and sugarcane plantations. In these initial migration years some Jamaicans also went to the USA, particularly New York, where some, like poet and author Claude McKay, played an important part in the rise of the Harlem Renaissance and various political movements. Marcus Garvey and Leonard Howell had migrated to the USA during this period. During the 1950s and into the early 1960s there was a mass exodus of Jamaicans to the United Kingdom, mainly for work with British Rail and London Transport. Jamaican independence from Britain in 1962 however resulted in restrictions on immigration to the UK, and the outward movement of Jamaican workers shifted towards the United States and Canada into cites such as New York, Miami and Toronto.

Many persons of Jamaican origin also now reside in other Caribbean countries, as well as in Central America and Europe. In more recent years there has also been a movement of Jamaican professionals to far away countries such as Australia, New Zealand, Japan, Malaysia and Indonesia. The result of the mass emigration from Jamaica over the past 100 years has been the creation of a Jamaican diaspora community which is estimated to be near equal in size to the Jamaican population resident on the island.

Cultural Impact and Influences from Migration

The arrival and settlement of Spanish explorers in Jamaica in the late 15th century resulted in almost total extinction of the indigenous Taino/Arawak inhabitants through the spread of diseases and war. There is therefore very little modern day evidence of the cultural influences of the original inhabitants of Jamaica. Spanish and subsequent British colonization have however significantly impacted Jamaican culture, particularly in the areas of religion, government, and language. The first capital of Jamaica was St Jago de la Vega, renamed SpanishTown by the British, as it was established during Spanish rule of the island. Many Spanish names of towns and streets across Jamaica can still be found, and Spanish Town holds a special place of significance. References to the first capital city and its famous prison appear in several songs by prominent artists – Spanish Town Prison Oval Rock by Barrington Levy[71]. and Two Sevens Clash by Culture.[72]

Jamaica's predominant Christian population is a result of the teachings of Spanish and British colonizers and the establishment of churches, initially of the Catholic and Anglican denominations. Jamaica currently has the third largest English speaking population in the Western Hemisphere, behind the USA and Canada, and is governed by laws and a political system based on the British Westminster model.

The African slave trade and the arrival and settlement of tribes from West, Central and East Africa has had the most significant impact on Jamaican culture and lifestyle. Today, persons of African descent account for 76 percent of the Jamaican population, and persons of mixed Afro-European descent account for another 15 percent. The African roots of Jamaican culture are very evident in religious and medicinal practices, music, dance, language and food that were transported from Africa by

71. https://www.youtube.com/watch?v=v_LpDBVM2Oo
72. https://www.youtube.com/watch?v=F3HITsh2vjE

slaves. This includes forms of religion where healing was regarded as an act of faith executed by obeah men, and communication with the spirits often induced by dancing and drumming. African based religious practices in Jamaica include Kumina and Revival, which incorporated the recreational, ceremonial and functional use of music and dance. Enslaved Africans in Jamaica recreated instruments from their motherland from materials such as calabash, conch and bamboo. African drumming for recreational and ceremonial activities, as well as for communication, although restricted by colonial laws since the 1600s to forestall their use in uprisings against slavery, played a significant part in developing Jamaican cultural activities.

Jamaican creole music was heavily influenced by African drumming and rhythms brought by slaves to the colonial plantations. As previously mentioned, the drumming traditions of East African Nyabinghi warriors played a very significant role in the emergent Jamaican Rastafari movement, as well as the creation of Reggae and other Jamaican music genres. Today's Jamaican music has evolved from the traditional work songs and ceremonial music used by African slaves in religious services and recreational activities. Aspirations for African unity, political and social development, have consistently provided a source of inspiration for the lyrical themes of music created in Jamaica over the years.

In addition to the musical influences that were introduced to Jamaica through slavery, African languages also figure prominently in Jamaican Creole or Patwa (Patois). The comunication between Africans and British English-speakers on the island resulted in the creation of a Creole that at one end is a Standard English and at the other, closer to some West African languages in grammatical structure, but dominated by English words and some African retentions. Since Patwa began to be formed in the 17th century, it has also been influenced by the languages of indentured workers brought to Jamaica from India and China, as well as settlers who came from Germany, France and Spain. Patwa is prominent in most modern Jamaican religious, folk and popular music.

Jamaican emigration to Central America, the UK, the USA, Canada and other countries has resulted in the emergence of a Jamaican diaspora with significant domestic and external cultural influences. This has been the major reason for the spread and growth of Jamaican music around the world.

The emigration of Jamaicans to Central America up to the 1920s, resulted in the creation of communities of people of Jamaican origin in countries such as Panama, Colombia (San Andres), Nicaragua and Costa Rica. There is much evidence of cultural retention in these communities today in the form of Jamaican influenced music and language. Popular Colombian group ChocQuib Town is a perfect example[73].

Migration has produced large communities of people of Jamaican origin in and around cities such as London, New York, Miami, and Toronto. Jamaican music, Patwa, and other cultural practices have become commonplace, and are an accepted part of daily life in these communities. Many non-Jamaicans in these communities have embraced the Jamaican lifestyle. Frequent travel by families and friends between Jamaica and the overseas Jamaican communities in the UK and North America has been the norm since the mid-20th century. This continuing movement in and out has aided the development and growth of trade in Jamaican goods and services as well as the spread of ideas and cultural practices.

A major Jamaican cultural effect of emigration has been the global presence of Rastafari. Rastafari culture is now prevalent in many countries around the world, with significant numbers of individuals, as well as some established organizations in the UK, Europe, the United States and the Caribbean. The focus of Rastafari culture on Africa, the close association between Rasta and Jamaican music, and the movement of Africans in and out of Europe, have also led to the presence of Rastafari on the African continent.

Global Reggae Influences

Jamaican emigration over the past 100 years has influenced the development of several new music genres around the world. Pop music culture in Latin America, North America, the UK and Europe have all experienced the development of genres and sub-genres of music influenced by the importation and adaptation of recognized Jamaican music genres such as Reggae, Ska and Dancehall.

Reggaeton

The Latin American community is now famous for Reggaeton, a music genre based on Latin and Jamaican music, derived from what was

---

73. https://www.youtube.com/watch?v=yMS4J6Gp6e4

originally called Reggae en Espanol originating in Panama. The genre was popularized in Puerto Rico where it also got its name, and most of its current artists are from Puerto Rico. The genre came to international prominence through the success in the USA of artists such as Daddy Yankee with his breakthrough hit Gasolina in 2004.[74] Gasolina and other formative North American Reggaeton hits also caught the attention of music fans in Europe, Asia and Africa.

Reggaeton is a fusion of musical influences from Jamaican Dancehall with genres from Latin America and the Caribbean such as Salsa, Bomba and Soca. While it takes its main influences from Jamaican Dancehall, Reggeton is not exactly the Hispanic or Latin American version of the Jamaican genre. Reggaeton has developed its own rhythmic flavour. The beat that characterizes Reggaeton was derived from a Jamaican recording by Shabba Ranks in the early 1990s called Dem Bow which was included on his album Just Reality.

Popular Jamaican music was introduced to Panama and the rest of Central America by Jamaican migrants who travelled mainly to work on the Panama Canal. Panama introduced Reggae en Espanol, and this music form made its way through Central America into the Caribbean, coming to prominence in Puerto Rico, where it became known as Reggaeton. Groundbreaking successes in Reggae en Espanol include recordings by El General and Nando Boom. El General is considered the father of Reggae en Espanol.[75] Puerto Rican rapper Vico C who released and promoted Reggaeton recordings in the 1980s, is credited as the pioneer in spreading the Reggaeton sound.

Since 2004 Reggaeton has gained widespread popularity in the United States and Europe with international hits by artists such as Tego Calderon, Don Omar, Ivy Queen, Luny Tunes, Noriega, Calle 13, Wisin & Yandel, Pit Bull and Tito El Bambino. The genre has gained significant recognition particularly within the United States mainstream music market, but has not had the same impact in Europe, where it is mostly popular in immigrant Latin American communities and in Spain. Reggaeton's popularity in the USA has influenced the formation of what is commonly referred to as Hurban radio, a combination of Hispanic and Urban music

---

74. https://www.youtube.com/watch?v=qGKrc3A6HHM
75. https://www.youtube.com/watch?v=NNWRCWkRr84

cultures. Like Reggae and Dancehall, Reggaeton'e themes also relate to many of the socio-economic issues affecting minorities in America.

Hip-Hop/Rap:

This music form is recognized primarily as an American originated music genre that is characterized by rhythmic music styles frequently accompanied by a rhythmic and rhyming speech called rapping. Traditional expressions of Hip-Hop music typically also incorporate scratching, sampling and beat boxing. Hip-Hop has also grown to include and encompass singing. There are Hip-Hop songs today that include very little or no rapping. Hip-Hop has evolved to become a culture and sub-culture incorporating lifestyle elements such as fashion.

In the 1970s residents of African American communities in sections of the Bronx in New York initiated what became known as house parties. Jamaican immigrants in these communities played a very important role in providing the musical entertainment for these parties through DJs playing popular music such as funk and soul. The practice of isolating the rhythmic breaks of the songs played by the DJs became a feature of house parties, and set the stage for the birth of the Hip-Hop music genre. The first exponents of this technique were persons with Jamaican connections, as it was already being practiced by sound system DJs in and around Kingston, in what became known worldwide as Dub music. As was the case in Jamaica, the emphasis of highlighting, juggling, sampling and mixing beats created the base for performers to rap in a manner identified as the art of toasting.

Jamaican immigrant Clive "Kool Herc" Campbell is credited as being the first exponent of Hip-Hop music. DJ Kool Herc, as he was called, is responsible for creating the style that became the blueprint for Hip-Hop music, by focusing on the short heavily percussive part in the recordings, called the "break". He also contributed to developing the rhyming style of Hip-Hop, by interjecting slangs and phrases to the breaks. For his contribution he is referred to as a "founding father of Hip-Hop". He provided inspiration for many other Americans of Jamaican origin who became major influencers of Hip-Hop.

Initially, Hip-Hop music was an outlet and a space for expression for disenfranchised youth of low economic areas in America, and reflected the social, economic and political realities of their lives, in a manner similar to Jamaican Reggae. In the late 1970s another Hi-Hop pioneer of Jamaican descent Kevin Donovan a.k.a. Afrika Bambaataa, emerged on the scene under the influence of DJ Kool Herc. Afrika Bambaataa brought to Hip-Hop lyrical content and an approach that sought to influence black youths against gangs and bring them closer to their African roots. After a visit to Africa, Donovan adopted the name Afrika Bambaataa, and formed what became known in Hip-Hop culture as the Zulu Nation. The Zulu Nation became the first Hip-Hop organization in 1977. Its mission was to build a movement to liberate and empower disenfranchised youths through their musical creativity.

The list of Jamaican immigrants to the USA, and descendants of immigrants who have participated in the formative years of Hip-Hop, reads almost like a "Who's Who" of early Rap music, and includes the following:

Luther Roderick Campbell, a.k.a. Luke Skywalker, or Luke, who became a Miami based record label owner, rap performer, and was best known as a member of 2 Live Crew. [76]

Lawrence Krisna Parker, a.k.a. KRS-One, a Bronx based rapper who in 2008 received from the BET Awards the Lifetime Achievement Award for his work in the Stop the Violence Movement, as well as his pioneering efforts to establish Hip-Hop music and culture. [77]

Christopher George Latore Wallace, a.k.a. The Notorious B.I.G., Biggie or Biggie Smalls, an American rapper of Jamaican parentage from Brooklyn, New York. He became a central figure in the East Coast Hip-Hop scene in the early 1990s.[78]

Dwight Errington Myers, a.k.a. Heavy D, a Jamaican born rapper, producer, singer, actor, who rose in the business to become the first rapper to head a major music label when he became president of Uptown Records. While at Uptown Records Heavy D was responsible for the hiring of Sean "Diddy" Combs in his first music business job as an intern.[79]

Dub Music and Jamaican Sound Systems

Dub music is a genre or sub-genre which evolved out of Reggae in

---

76. https://www.youtube.com/watch?v=nEH_ms8d1ws
77. https://www.youtube.com/watch?v=Z-alEhlHSzk
78. https://www.youtube.com/watch?v=_JZom_gVfuw
79. . https://www.youtube.com/watch?v=NNEgUPKxk7A

the 1960s. Jamaican Dub music was introduced to the UK by migrants and visitors from the island, and has developed to extend way beyond the scope of Reggae over the past several decades.

Original Jamaican Dub music was pioneered by music producers and studio recording engineers such as Osbourne "King Tubby" Ruddock, Lee "Scratch" Perry, Errol Thompson, and Hopeton "Scientist" Brown. Dub music is based on instrumental remixes of existing recordings, and incorporates the manipulation and reshaping of these recordings by removing all or sections of the vocals and other music tracks, and emphasizing the drum and bass. The extensive use and addition of echo, reverb, delay and other effects is also a significant feature of Dub recordings. King Tubby is regarded as the father of dub music.[80]

In the 1970s and 1980s the UK became a new center of Dub Music production with the influence of individuals such as Mikey Dread, Mad Professor, and Jah Shaka. The works of these pioneers in the UK led to music production collaborations, and also had significant influence on the music of British artists such as UB40, The Clash, and The Police. Since the 1980s Dub music in the UK, and by extension Europe, has been influenced by and has in turn influenced several newer music genres and sub-genres such as Punk, Drum and Bass, Techno, Jungle, Dubstep, and House Music.

The Jamaican sound system phenomenon has also been exported by emigrants from the Island over the past several decades, leading to major musical influences in the UK, Europe, USA and Japan. A Jamaican sound system comprises turntables (now CD mixers and computers), speakers, a PA system, a deejay and a selector. The deejay in sound system culture is not to be confused with the American term DJ, which refers to the person in charge of selecting the music at an event where recorded music is played. The sound system deejay is the person who speaks on the mic, while the person who selects music on a sound system is called the selector.

Sound systems have existed in Jamaica from the opening days of the development of Jamaican popular music, and have played a very important role in the advancement of Dub music. Without established sound systems Dub music would not be nearly as popular or as developed as it is today. Dub music provided the soundtrack for deejays to experiment and

---

80. .   https://www.youtube.com/watch?v=ZvYSYOKFCbk

improvise with vocal overlays in the dance halls, and eventually in the recording studios. Sound systems have evolved to become massive production sets to include large and sophisticated computerized equipment and crew with capacity to tour and perform worldwide. Many deejays, DJs and selectors have also evolved to become popular music producers and performing artists themselves on the mainstream global music scene.

Exploiting Reggae's Global Impact

Migration and advances in technology have greatly facilitated the wide global presence of Reggae music, and have placed Jamaica in a unique and favorable position. Opportunities for the international marketing of Reggae are many, particularly in countries in Europe, the Caribbean, North, South and Central America, and Africa. For several decades Jamaican artists and music producers have done well to take advantage of the European and North American markets for Reggae. In recent years they have had to compete with home-grown European and North American Reggae artists who have been doing better business in both recorded music sales and live performances. The Caribbean market continues to be a lucrative market for Jamaican live music presentations, but markets such as Africa, Central and South America remain grossly under-exploited by Jamaicans. The case of the Central and South American market for Reggae requires special attention in light of the size of that market and the impact of Reggaeton.

The Jamaican diaspora is reported to be as large as the size of its home population, but engagement with the diaspora has not been as effective or as structured as it should be. The complexity of the music industry, and the wide scale global presence of Reggae necessitates the deployment of a specialized international strategy within the Jamaican government's Ministry of Foreign Affairs and Trade. It is advisable that such a strategy should include collaboration with the Ministry of Tourism and Entertainment and the Jamaica Promotions Corporation/JAMPRO. There should be a Jamaica Music Export Office with a qualified international trade representative.

Brain Drain, Globalization, or Brain Freeze
– Facebook note, October 2009 [81]

A few days ago the mail woman delivered to my home in South Florida my Permanent Resident (Green Card) notice from the United States Citizenship and Immigration Service. Among other things, the notice read: "Welcome to the United States of America". I was immediately plunged into a state of deep reflection.

I reflected on the fact that the most beautiful island in the Caribbean has more of its people living outside of it than the entire population of Trinidad and Tobago, Barbados and other Eastern Caribbean islands put together. I also reflected on the fact that it was the enterprise and courage of Jamaicans living away from home that contributed to the building of the Panama Canal, and that if it were not for the inspiration and efforts of "runaway" Jamaicans like Marcus Garvey, Leonard Howell, Arthur Wint, and Don Taylor, where would Usain Bolt, Bob Marley, Rastafari and Reggae be today.

Globalization describes an ongoing process by which regional economies, societies, and cultures have become integrated through a globe-spanning network of communication and exchange. It is fair to say that the entire world population is bewildered at the accomplishments of Jamaica – "The biggest little country in the world". Yes, that's who we are, or as my friend Dr. Leahcim Semaj says, "A world super power". Jamaicans have been practicing globalization for decades.

The reasons why Jamaicans leave their homeland are many and varied. I was forced to venture outward after feeling the oppression and rejection of a rapacious financial system that seized control of my home and then my business place. I was also very discouraged by the ingratitude and lack of appreciation I experienced after a quarter of a century of contribution to local music industry development.

I have always struggled to understand the concept of brain drain, as used in the Jamaican context. I do know what brain freeze is however. I would liken brain freeze to a "dead-stock" computer

---

81. https://www.facebook.com/notes/lloyd-stanbury/brain-drain-globalization-or-brain-freeze/10154428876365355

that keeps freezing when you need to get work done, which reminds me of many Jamaican political and business leaders today. They are stuck in the dark ages. While spouting off about globalization, the political leadership of Jamaica remains undecided on whether Jamaican political and government representation should include persons who live outside the Island.

It's full time we come to grips with the fact that Jamaica is bigger than the island in the Caribbean Sea, and that the Jamaican community is truly a global one.

With Jamaica's long tradition of migration, a very influential and widespread Diasporic community has been created. This community has made an indelible mark on popular music worldwide, and created one of Jamaica's most valuable assets, its musical culture. The failure of leaders and policy makers in government and the private sector to develop partnerships and strategies to enable more effective management and exploitation of this asset, has without question stifled further development of the business of Reggae locally and internationally.

Is Jamaican Reggae Struggling to Survive in the USA?
– Facebook note, April 22, 2013 [82]

The US music market is the single largest in the world, and accounts for a significant portion of global recorded music sales as well as live performance income. While many will argue that the American music industry is representative of the "Babylon System", and that Jamaican artists should look to other markets such as Africa, I do think we need to also take some time to examine the situation that has resulted in the following:

1. A recent news report by a mainstream US television network posted online made the observation that the Billboard Reggae Top 10 albums charts of a few weeks ago had seven artists in the top ten who were non-Jamaicans [83]

2. The recently concluded Austin Reggae Festival (April 19 -21)

82. https://www.facebook.com/notes/lloyd-stanbury/is-jamaican-Reggae-struggling-to-survive-in-the-usa/10153170127710355

83. http://www.erietvnews.com/video?autoStart=true&topVideoCatNo=default&clipId=8740458

is said to have had its largest crowd turn out in its 20 years of staging. Estimates are that between 25,000 and 30,000 persons attended the festival. My review of the Main Stage line-up for Austin Reggae Festival 2013 revealed that only one Jamaican band (The Wailers) was featured at the event this year, out of a total of 16 bands. [84]

There has been a whole lot of talk over the years in Jamaica about policies and strategies for development of the Jamaican music industry and the broader cultural and creative industries. Unfortunately there has been much talk and very little meaningful action.

It is my view that creative industries development in Jamaica should be pursued in the context of our competitive advantage as clearly demonstrated by the global brand acceptance of Reggae music and all its associated products and services. The US music market is not the only market of significance, but it happens to be the single largest music market in the world, the nearest to Jamaica, and the one in which we perhaps have the largest number of Jamaicans who live away from home.

In my opinion, we cannot seriously address the issue of creative industries development in Jamaica without taking time to do necessary research to arrive at answers and solutions to the challenges exemplified by the Austin Reggae Festival and the Billboard Reggae Top 10 albums charts. Lessons learned from such a research exercise are likely to prove very valuable in our efforts to address the capacity building and market access considerations for an effective creative industries development policy and implementation plan.

Is the Internet Killing Payola in Jamaica?
– Facebook note, November 24, 2013 [85]

I have had a long association with music producers, recording artists and media personalities in Jamaica, and one of the most vexed issues in any discussion about the development of Jamaica's

---

84. http://austinReggaefest.com

85. https://www.facebook.com/notes/lloyd-stanbury/is-the-internet-killing-Payola-in-jamaica/10154021666920355

music industry has always been Payola. For those of us who do not know, Payola is the acceptance by media operators (mainly radio personalities), of favours in exchange for their promotion and exposure of the music and other activities of recording artists. Payola is typically a secret activity conducted by media personnel, usually without the knowledge of management of the media house in question. In the USA this activity has been made illegal.

Under U.S. law, 47 U.S.C.§ 317, a radio station can play a specific song in exchange for money, but this must be disclosed on the air as being sponsored airtime, and that play of the song should not be counted as "regular airplay". If there is pay for play without disclosure there is an infringement of the law.

While there has been much debate about Payola in Jamaica there is still no law in place to address the issue. I have had very personal and direct experiences of Payola in the Jamaican music industry, both from my vantage point of a media executive at IRIE FM, and as the representative of several Jamaican artists and music producers. One would be amazed at how sophisticated the Payola "racket" has become in Jamaica, and many do not realize the extent of the damage this activity has done to our music.

With the advent of the Internet and in particular social media sites such as Facebook, YouTube, SoundCloud etc., many Jamaican artists have been using these alternative means of promoting their music. There are now several artists who have been able to successfully promote their careers and music without having to rely on the sometimes parasitic behavior of corrupt local media practitioners and their agents. The practice of Payola in Jamaica became so rampant that actual businesses have been established and operated by persons who rely on Payola for their existence. This new trend towards use of new technologies for music exposure has without doubt posed a serious threat to the Payola business in Jamaica. The rise of the Reggae Revival movement and the international recognition gained by several of the emerging artists associated with this movement is a direct testament to the effectiveness of the Internet and social media as the new alternative music promotion vehicle.

Unfortunately, there are still some artists and music producers who continue to believe that they must subject themselves to the abuse of corrupt media practitioners to get ahead. I would however encourage them to look beyond the narrow local media landscape, and extend themselves to access the wider global market with the help of the Internet and social media.

Summary

- Movement in and out of Jamaica of persons of African, European, East Indian and American origin has had a very significant impact on the development of Jamaican culture and music.
- Migration of Jamaicans has facilitated the increased popularity of Jamaican music in foreign countries, particularly in Europe, the Caribbean, North and Central America.
- Migration and the flow of information have enabled many non-Jamaicans to learn to produce Reggae and other Jamaican music forms.
- Reggae produced and performed by non-Jamaicans often enjoys greater market success in international markets than Reggae produced and presented by Jamaicans.
- Jamaican music genres have given birth to popular music genres such as Hip Hop and Reggaeton.
- Many Jamaican artists, music producers and managers have not mastered the use of the Internet and other new communication technologies as marketing tools.
- Innovative Jamaican audio engineering and sound reinforcement technology and practices evident in dub music and sound systems have resulted in globally accepted techniques such as re-mixing, and the use of studio recording effects.

Government and the Music Industry

Jamaica, like many other developing countries, is characterized by the existence of poor economic conditions alongside a rich supply of raw materials and human talent capable of being commercially exploited in more developed nations. In the case of the Jamaican music industry, there exists a large pool of creative talent that has produced artists and musical works with phenomenal impact and influence on international popular culture. The emergence of new digital and communication technologies have facilitated greater levels of interaction locally and globally, thus enabling more opportunities for growth of the creative and commercial potential of Jamaican music. These circumstances also dictate that Government should of necessity act in partnership with participants of the music industry to design and implement appropriate industry development policies and strategies.

What Constitutes the Music Industry

In order that agencies of government can effectively interact and facilitate music industry development, it is necessary that representatives of these agencies have some basic understanding of what is involved in the processes of production, promotion and distribution of music goods and services. In this chapter of REGGAE ROADBLOCKS, and those following, we will define the music industry by identifying the main segments and key functionaries, and describing them as best we can.

The music industry refers to the business activities connected with the creation, performance, recording, presentation, transmission and sale of sound recordings and live performances. It consists of musicians, vocalists, songwriters, music producers, audio engineers, record companies, labels, music publishers, recording studios, and support service providers such as show promoters, booking agents, artist managers, publicists, designers, technicians, entertainment attorneys, and technical suppliers. For the purposes of this book we will categorize the various activities in the music industry under three broad heads:

1. Sound Recordings, or the recording industry
2. Live Performance Services and Events
3. Associated Merchandise and Branding, Other Services, and Media Content

Sound Recordings

The sound recording business or recording industry as it is often called, consists of those activities surrounding the writing and recording of songs, and the promotion, distribution, sale, public performance, and broadcasting to the public of recordings of these songs in various formats, ranging from physical records, CDs, and tapes, to digital music transmitted via the Internet and mobile communication devices. The business relationships between the songwriters, vocal performers, musicians, music producers, distributors and broadcasters of sound recordings are typically governed by a combination of provisions within copyright law and/or contracts between the relevant parties.

Live Performance Services and Events

The business of live music consists primarily of the provision by artists of music performances, and the promotion and presentation of events by show promoters for public consumption. In recent years live music has taken on more significance as a primary revenue stream for the music industry. This added significance is the result of annual rates of decline in sound recording sales experienced globally in recent years, as reported by the International Federation for the Phonographic Industry (IFPI). Apart from performers, show promoters and producers, there are several other participants in the live music industry, ranging from providers of technical services such as venue rental, sound reinforcement, lighting, stage and set construction, to stage management, tour management, and performance bookings.

Associated Merchandise, Branding, Other Services, Media Content

Associated music merchandise and branding, other services and media content, refers to activities and items such as branded clothing and accessories associated with music and artists, music in advertising, artist endorsements, music in video games, and audio-visual music related media content such as promotional music videos, and music programmes produced for radio, television, and Internet broadcast. These have all become significant sources of business and revenue for music industry operators around the world. In addition to being a source of revenue, audio-visual music programmes such as promotional music videos and documentaries have become essential marketing tools for sound recordings and artists.

The Role of Government in Music Industry Development

For many years there have been debates inside Jamaica about the role and impact of Government in relation to music industry development. While some argue and defend the extreme position that government involvement is unwanted interference, others complain that not enough is being done by government in the form of policy and implementation strategies to support structured industry growth. An analysis of the role of government should however be done against the background of a clear understanding of what constitutes the components of the music industry, who the key functionaries are, and what roles do they play. There is wide scale misunderstanding in Jamaica with regard to the roles to be played by various necessary individual and institutional operatives in the music industry.

The role and effectiveness of the Jamaican government in music industry development should be examined and measured in the context of the following key result areas:

- Product and service supply
- Organizational infrastructure

- Investments
- Domestic market development
- Regional and international market development
- Professional development and training Regulation and policy, and
- Linkages with sectors such as tourism, communications, and digital technologies.

The question to be answered is how successful have Jamaican government administrations been in designing policies and implementing strategies to positively impact the above result areas in the music industry. To provide an appropriate answer it is imperative that one takes into account the historical factors surrounding the development of Jamaican music. One must also consider the domestic and global impact of the island's music, particularly in relation to its influence on popular music culture around the world.

Jamaican music and artists were highlighted as far back as the mid-1950s when Harry Belafonte's album Calypso became the first million selling record in the history of popular music. The recognition and acceptance of Bob Marley as an icon in pop music culture is also great testimony to the importance of Jamaican music and its global commercial viability. When these and other issues are considered, it is my conclusion that the government administrations in Jamaica have failed miserably in their role as facilitators of music industry development.

Since the 1990s Jamaica's music industry has been the subject of several studies and reports conducted by local and international economists, industry experts, university professors, and trade development agencies. During this period, I have been exposed to and/or participated in more than ten studies regarding various aspects of the development of Jamaica's music industry. These have included reports and research papers facilitated by and/or presented to agencies such as the Planning Institute of Jamaica, the University of the West Indies, the Jamaican Ministry of Culture, Jamaica Promotions Corporation (JAMPRO), The World Intellectual Property Organization (WIPO), the United Nations Conference on Trade and Development (UNCTAD), the United Nations Development Programme (UNDP), as well as industry development initiatives funded by the European Union. The CARICOM affiliated Caribbean Export Development Agency based in Barbados has also commissioned several studies on the music industries of the region and hosted trade development workshops and conferences.

It could therefore be successfully argued that as a sector, Jamaica's music industry has been studied and reported on more than any other sector of the local economy in the past two decades. Despite this, there is relatively little evidence of any effective national policies or actions taken by government to facilitate the development of a structured local industry.

In my opinion, the issue of copyright administration is one of the very few areas where the Jamaican government could be credited with a pass grade as a facilitator. The passage of a new Copyright Act in 1993, and the establishment of the Jamaica Intellectual Property Office (JIPO) in 2001, have without doubt provided necessary supportive regulatory infrastructure for the development of Jamaica's music industry.

In April 2015 a long awaited Bill to amend the Jamaican Copyright Act was tabled in Parliament.[86] Other government interventions have however been slow and ad hoc, and have been hampered by a preoccupation with the excuse that local music industry private sector operators have been disorganized and have continued to operate in an environment of fragmentation.

Jamaica's education policy as it relates to capacity building in the area of music and arts management has also been woefully inadequate, despite the fact that many of the studies conducted identify music business management deficiency as the greatest barrier to industry development in Jamaica. In addition, while dedicating significant amounts of financial resources and time to tourism and information and communication technology development, Jamaican government policies have failed to effectively capitalize on the benefits to be had from strategic linkages between the music industry and these other sectors of the economy. Government policy on local and international broadcast of entertainment content has been weak and somewhat misguided. The tendency of the Broadcasting Commission of Jamaica has been to respond to overseas pressure to protect foreign copyrights, rather than act in defense of the rights of local content producers at home and abroad.[87]

For many years various representatives of government in Jamaica

---

86. http://www.jamaicaobserver.com/news/Copyright-Amendment-Bill-Tabled_18785801
87. http://jamaica-gleaner.com/article/news/20150424/49-cable-companies-breaching-copyright-laws

have made announcements and engaged in discussions with regard to the design of a national policy and the implementation of strategies for the development of the cultural and creative industries. Unfortunately these discussions have not to date produced either a policy or strategy for structured music industry development. Many regard these government representations as mere political announcements aimed at generating publicity, as they are typically made during annual budget presentations and rallies at election campaigns, with very little if any meaningful follow up.

Creative Industries

There have been some attempts by the Jamaican government to establish dedicated agencies charged with the responsibility of providing guidance and advice in the areas of creative industry and entertainment industry development. The Creative Industries Unit within the Jamaica Promotions Corporation (JAMPRO), and the Entertainment Industry Advisory Board, within the Ministry of Tourism and Entertainment are two such examples. The effectiveness and impact of most government initiatives have however been very limited, as they are often structured to rely on voluntary boards and committees with inadequate budgetary allocations for their operations. In the 2015 presentation of the Government's budget of expenditures, it was stated that entertainment and music would receive a significant increase over prior years.[88]

In March 2014, Jamaican Prime Minister Portia Simpson Miller convened the first meeting of the National Cultural and Creative Industries Commission, as a follow up to an announcement made more than one year earlier. The Commission is to be supported by a technical working group administered within the Office of the Prime Minister. The Commission is mandated to develop a national cultural and creative industries policy and a master plan for the sustainable development of the sector. The assumption is that this national policy and master plan will also include policies and strategies for the sustainable development of the music industry.

The establishment of a National Cultural and Creative Industries Commission with supporting technical experts within the Office of the Jamaican Prime Minister represents a move in the right direction. This

---

88. http://jamaica-gleaner.com/article/entertainment/20150302/budget-increase-entertainment

initiative will however fail if it is not implemented with adequate funding, and staffed with appropriate technical experts. In her first meeting with the members of the Commission, the Prime Minister is quoted as saying:

"We need to recognize how important these industries are for both economic growth and national   development imperatives".

Only time will tell whether these are mere lofty words, or a demonstration of the required political will to make a difference. There is a very strong sentiment among many within and outside the music industry that the government of Jamaica will never provide the required support to facilitate the development of a local music industry. This position is based on the view that for decades Reggae and other forms of Jamaican music have produced performers and songwriters who consistently speak out against the injustices, discrimination, and disrespect suffered by African Jamaican descendants of slaves at the hands of pre and post-colonial Jamaican governments.

If the National Cultural and Creative Industries Commission is to be a success, the issues outlined above will have to be confronted and addressed. It will also be necessary for the Commission or some off-shoot from the Commission to evolve or merge with an existing entity to become a statutory government corporation or other legal entity established under the Companies Act of Jamaica to give it some degree of permanence. The significance of the global market to the development of the Jamaican music and creative industries also dictates that any permanent off-shoot from the Commission should be established with appropriate representation outside of Jamaica, similar to the external representation enjoyed by other government industry development agencies such as the Jamaica Tourist Board, and Jamaica Promotions Corporation (JAMPRO).

Despite all the studies and recommendations made, and despite the proven ability of Jamaican music performers and producers to compete globally and come out on top, Jamaica was still without a defined national policy and strategic plan for music industry development in March 2015, one year after the Prime Minister convened the first meeting of the National Cultural and Creative Industries Commission convened by the Prime Minister. The National Cultural Policy of 2003, prepared by the Jamaican Ministry of Youth and Culture is not enough, as it is a cultural policy document only. What is needed is a strategic plan for the development of Jamaica's creative and cultural industries, including music.

The inability of the Jamaican Government to effectively address the issue of comprehensive, structured and sustainable development of the music industry is largely due to the fact that the cultural and creative industries have never been treated as top priority in any national development plan. Adequate resources have never been allocated for the establishment of a dedicated ministry or government department charged with responsibility for cultural and creative industries development. Instead government's responsibility to facilitate development in this sector has been shared by several ministries and departments which often compete with each other rather than cooperate and collaborate. This has resulted in a great degree of overlap and ineffective use of state funds.

If I Were the Jamaican Minister of Culture
– Facebook note: Tuesday, December 14, 2010[89]

The role of government in cultural industries development has been a topic of much debate when it comes to Jamaica. One view that is constantly put forward by some is that government should have nothing to do with music industry development. With all due respect to those who continue to hold that view, it is my opinion that your position is one based on ignorance. Sorry to be so harsh, but the facts speak for themselves, if we take the time to examine what has worked for cultural industries that thrive in other countries around the globe.

I am not by any means considering a position in government in Jamaica, as indeed I think I would be a lonely soldier among a group of self-serving politicians who lack vision and creativity. If however I were to dream of being the Minister of Culture in Jamaica, this is what I would wish to see:

1. The Edna Manley College for the Visual and Performing Arts be adequately funded and supported in order to expand its curriculum offerings and physical facilities to include more

---

89.https://www.facebook.com/notes/lloyd-stanbury/if-i-were-the-jamaican-minister-of-cul-ture/10150353356725355

emphasis on courses focused on arts and entertainment management and entrepreneurship.

2. The Broadcasting Commission get some teeth, and come up with appropriate recommendations and measures to contain the scourge of Payola.

3. The Jamaica Tourist Board includes the development of indigenous local culture as an essential and priority aspect of its programme for the enhancement of the local tourism product. We are more than sand and sea and lovely hotel buildings. Our music is also not Jamaica Jazz and Blues.

4. The inclusion of music education and appreciation courses as part of the curriculum in primary, secondary and tertiary institutions, with appropriate support facilities such as musical instruments and tutors who recognize and appreciate the value of local music.

5. The provision of tax incentives to encourage local and international entrepreneurs to invest in production, training and presentation of local music on the Island.

Some of us may ask why it has not been possible to implement the above suggestions when the fact is they are not by any means new ones. These and similar ideas have been presented to government in Jamaica time and time again over the past two decades. In my view one reason these measures have not been implemented has to do with the fact that the Ministry of Culture does not seem to have a say in, or any significant influence over, what is done by the Ministry of Information as regards the Broadcasting Commission, or the Ministry of Tourism with regard to how tourism promotion dollars are spent. The Jamaican Ministry of Culture has also apparently not been able to affect decision making within the Ministries of Industry and Commerce and Education respectively, when it comes to tax incentive regulations or the developments within our formal educational system.

My dream as Minister of Culture would therefore have to include the establishment of a joint Ministerial body headed by the Culture Minister to oversee the policy making activities and budgetary allocations in the above mentioned Ministries in so far as they relate to and/or impact the development of cultural industries.

Summary

- There is inadequate understanding and appreciation by representatives of government regarding what constitutes the music industry.
- Education in arts and music business management needs to be given top priority.
- More effective linkages between music and the tourism and technology sectors need to be created.
- There is no evidence of an effective national development policy for Jamaica's music industry.
- There is need for a local broadcast policy that facilitates development and exposure of local entrainment content.
- Government's role in international negotiations related to trade in cultural goods and services needs to be more effective and guided by expert industry advice.
- Advisory bodies need to be funded, and less reliance placed on volunteers.
- Government ministries and agencies that impact the development of cultural industries need to consolidate and collaborate rather than compete and operate in silos.
- Tax incentives are required to encourage investors in the sector.

Sizzla Kalonji is a globally recognized Reggae and dancehall artist with a militant and outspoken personality. He is one of several prominent Jamaican artists who have experienced work permit and visa denials to enter North America and some European countries. © 2015 Sista Irie Photography

Queen Ifica is a very popular and outspoken artist whose firm stance on homosexuality has caused much controversy both locally and internationally. © 2015 Sista Irie Photography

Marcia Griffith is the undisputed queen of Jamaican popular music, with a very successful recording and performing career spanning over 5 decades. © 2014 Sista Irie Photography.

Etana "TheStrongOne", established herself as an excellent recording artist, performer and songwriter with music messages that relate to a cross section of issues at both the local and international level. © 2013 Sista Irie Photography

Tarrus Riley (son of Jimmy Riley), is one of several second generation Reggae artists to make a significant contribution to the resurgence of roots Reggae inside Jamaica since the turn of the century. © 2014 Sista Irie Photography

Chronixx has been the most significant new Jamaican artist to emerge on the local and international scene since the turn of the century, and is the most prominent artist identified with what some refer to as the "Reggae Revival". © 2015 Sista Irie Photography

Tessanne rose to international prominence in 2013 as the winner of Season 5 of the popular North American NBC TV programme "The Voice". She is regarded as one of the truly great female voices from Jamaica. © 2013 Sista Irie Photography

Jah9 is the most significant Rastafari female recording and performing artist to emerge from Jamaica in many years, and is also identified with the "Reggae Revival" movement. © 2013 Sista Irie Photography

140

Protoje is another second generation Jamaican recording artist (son of Lorna Bennett), and is hailed as the artist mostly responsible for the encouragement and development of the "Reggae Revival" movement. © 2013 Sista Irie Photography

Kabaka Pyramid is a very popular artist associated with the "Reggae Revival", and Is known for his lyrics with strong social and political commentaries mixed with roots Reggae, dancehall and Hip-Hop. © 2015 Sista Irie Photography

Kelissa is yet another second generation Jamaican recording artist (daughter of Errol "Chakula" McDonald, and "Goldilocks"). She is also closely associated with the "Reggae Revival" movement.
© 2015 Sista Irie Photography

Kumar Bent is lead singer and guitarist with the band Raging Fyah, and is hailed as one of the top young songwriters and vocalists in reggae.
© 2014 Sista Irie Photography

Alborosie is an Italian roots Reggae artist that has gained mainstream acceptance and popularity on the European Reggae circuit while also being highly respected in Jamaica. © 2015 Sista Irie Photography

Collie Buddz is a Bermudan Reggae artist who broke big on the North American Reggae music scene and also gained critical acclaim inside Jamaica. © 2013 Sista Irie Photography

Holly Cook is a British Reggae artist with strong musical roots (Daughter of Sex Pistols drummer Paul Cook and Jeni, a back up singer for Boy George's Culture Club). She is internationally known for her sultry soulful Reggae recordings and stage presentations. © 2014 Sista Irie Photography

Rocky Dawuni is a Ghanaian Reggae artist based in California. Seen here at Austin's live Reggae club Flamingo Cantina, during South By SouthWest Music Festival 2015. © 2015 Sista Irie Photography

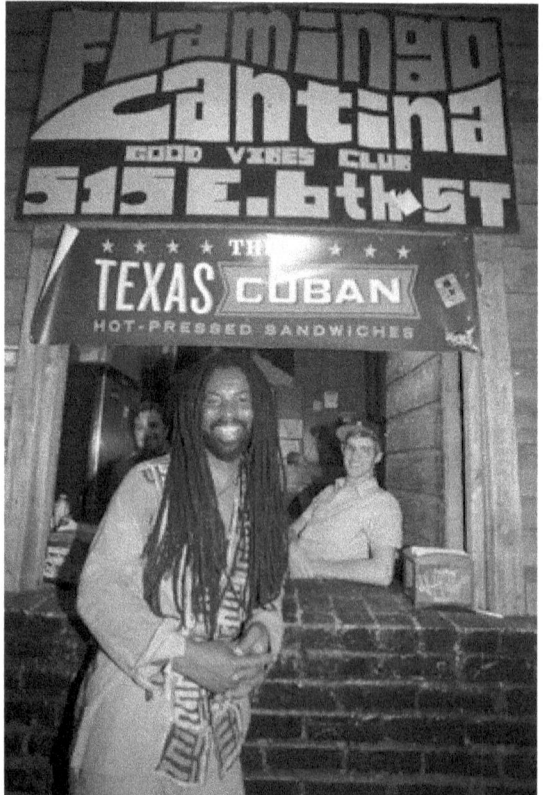

Interacting With National and International Music Industry Institutions

Regulation and performance measurement are critical components of industry development in the sphere of culture, as they are in other aspects of any economy. The music industry survives and thrives through the existence of an organized mechanism of domestic legislation, international conventions, and national and international trade and collective rights representation organizations. Interacting with, and ensuring the viability and efficiency of these institutions is critical to the development of the sector.

Unity and Collective Representation is the Key

One of the most commonly identified weaknesses of the Jamaican music industry has been the disunity and fragmentation that exists among its many participants. This is supported by several of the studies conducted, and is cited as a major barrier to industry development. Successive government administrations have also cited this weakness as the reason for their inability to develop and implement necessary policy and strategy.

The existence of properly structured and efficiently managed national music associations and institutions is an indispensable component of industry development. For example, properly run music industry associations play a very important role in generating economic data, such as employment and domestic and export income statistics. They also serve the purpose of providing a platform for lobbying, advocacy, education and awareness building for industry participants, as well as being vehicles for public education about the value and significance of the industry to social and economic development. The collective administration of the various rights of songwriters, performers, and music producers is another key function of music industry associations. Over the years Jamaica has struggled to establish and maintain fully functional and efficient music associations. As is the case with the performance of government, it may be argued that the greatest accomplishment for local music associations has been in the area of copyright and related rights administration.

Since the passage of the Jamaican Copyright Act 1993, much attention and focus has been directed at rights administration in the music industry. This has led to the establishment of the first national collective rights management organization for music in Jamaica in the form of the Jamaica Association of Composers Authors and Publishers (JACAP). JACAP was formed in 1998, and took over the role of collective rights management for songwriters and music publishers that was formerly handled by the UK based Performing Rights Society.

JACAP has managed to increase its songwriter and publisher membership and representation from under 1,000 to over 3,400 at the end of 2014, and has also contributed to building awareness among music practitioners and members of the Jamaican public regarding music copyrights. The organization however still suffers from internal management and governance weaknesses. JACAP's weaknesses and the lack of strong international advocacy and negotiating representation of Jamaican music copyrights, have hindered the conversion of the global popularity of Jamaican music to net inflows of revenues due from the public performance of Jamaican music by radio, TV and other users around the world. JACAP has also struggled to secure voluntary compliance from media operators in Jamaica who use music, and has been forced to initiate legal proceedings against several such entities.[90] There is a lack of a culture of compliance in Jamaica, as many regard music as being free for their personal use and public consumption.

In 2006 the Jamaica Music Society (JAMMS) was established as a collective management organization to globally represent the rights of

---

90. http://www.jamaicaobserver.com/news/Law-suits-fi ed-against-media-houses-for-copyright-breaches--more-to-come----JACAP

music producers. Since its formation JAMMS has worked very closely with international agencies such as the International Federation of the Phonographic Industry (IFPI), and the USA based Sound Exchange in the area of collective rights management pertaining to the public performance use of sound recordings.

Apart from JACAP and JAMMS, there have been several other initiatives pursued towards the establishment and operation of Jamaican music associations and institutions designed to facilitate industry development. The Jamaica Federation of Musicians Union (JFM), was established in 1958 under the Trade Unions Act of Jamaica, and is the oldest existing music organization in Jamaica. Its main purpose is to function as a trade union for musicians and other performers. Among the JFMs aims and objectives are the promotion of live music, the improvement of musical talent, improvement of working conditions, and   protection of the interests of all its members, the establishment and maintenance of uniform and fair prices for musicians and artists services, the provision of funds for old age grants, sick benefits, schools and other educational facilities for the use of, and catering to the needs of proponents of the musical art. Although the JFM has managed to remain in existence since 1958, and has established and maintained international relationships, the union has in recent years failed to generate adequate levels of membership participation, and has not been able to deliver on much of the aims and objectives outlined above. The Union has also suffered badly from very weak governance and internal administrative capacity, and has not been able to generate and maintain consistent levels of membership dues collections.

In 1990 the world's first all Reggae 24-hour terrestrial radio station IRIE FM, was launched in Ocho Rios Jamaica. IRIE FM was established and operated by Grove Broadcasting Company to provide a vehicle for the exposure and promotion of Reggae and other indigenous Jamaican music genres recorded by local and foreign artists. Included in the station's operational activities was the monthly staging of live concert events featuring established and emerging Reggae artists. The main objectives of the station were to expose the Jamaican public to high quality recorded and live music, and to encourage local artists to strive for internationally accepted music production standards.

As the co-founder and first vice-chairman of IRIE FM, it is my opinion that the station did well to achieve its objectives for the first five to ten years of its operation, but has since lost its focus. IRIE FM has now become one of the main facilitators of the Payola (pay for play) system in Jamaica that enables almost any kind of music to be aired without any regard whatsoever for quality.

Reggae's impact as a major influence on popular culture, as a catalyst for social and political change, and as a viable economic sector for Jamaica, is recognized and celebrated annually through the establishment of International Reggae Day on July 1st 1994. International Reggae Day is a global 24-hour media festival that encompasses a vast international network of online newspapers, magazines, radio stations and other web based platforms.[91]

A number of music associations and institutions have been formed in Jamaica that have either become dormant or fallen short in realizing their mandate. These include the Jamaica Performers Administration Society which was established as a collective rights management organization to represent public performance rights of sound recording performers such as vocalists and musicians. This organization has however been inactive for several years. The Recording Industry Association of Jamaica (RIAJam) was established in 2003 to represent the interests of individuals and companies operating in the Jamaican recording industry, such as music producers, record labels, music publishers, music distributors and manufacturers. RIAJam is responsible for the establishment of the Jamaica Music Society/JAMMS as well as the conceptualization of Reggae Month. In 2007 RIAJam made representation to the Government of Jamaica, and secured a formal declaration by Prime Minister Bruce Golding of February as Reggae Month. The first Reggae Month activities in February 2008 were coordinated by RIAJam. These included the staging of the inaugural Reggae Academy Awards in conjunction with the Reggae Academy, an international members-driven recording academy established by RIAJam. RIAJam has however remained dormant since the successful staging of the Reggae Academy Awards in 2008.

In 2004 the Jamaica Association of Vintage Artists and Affiliates (JAVAA) was formed with a stated mission to preserve the rich musical history of Jamaica, and to protect the professional and social well-being

---

91. http://www.billboard.com/biz/articles/news/global/1177237/international-Reggae-day-cele-brated-across-the-globe

of the vintage artists and musicians. One of JAVAA's main projects has been the JAVAA Jamaica Music Hall of Fame, which had its first inductees in 2008.

In the latter part of the year 2008 the Jamaica Reggae Industry Association (JaRIA) was formed in response to the decision taken by RIAJam to place on hold the staging of the annual Reggae Academy Awards, due to lack of government and other necessary corporate sponsorship support. JaRIA was mandated by then Minister of Culture Olivia "Babsy" Grange to assume responsibility for the Reggae Month initiative, and has continued to act as the secretariat for the organization and presentation of annual Reggae Month celebrations and activities in Jamaica. JaRIA has also positioned itself to become an umbrella organization to represent the interests of several music associations now operating in Jamaica, and includes JACAP, JAVAA and JAMMS among its members.

The performance of national music associations in Jamaica has been adversely affected by wide-scale mistrust and ignorance about the intricacies of the business of music that persists among the majority of industry participants. There is also an inadequate supply of qualified administrators, which has resulted in the tendency of creative practitioners to assume administrative roles for which they are not sufficiently qualified. The partisan political allegiance of administrators of music organizations has also adversely impacted their credibility and effectiveness. Weak and ineffective Jamaican music associations and institutions will continue to present roadblocks to the development of the Reggae music industry. Weak institutions hinder the establishment of necessary partnerships between the state and private sector music industry operators, and prevent effective partnerships between local practitioners and their international counterparts.

Interacting With International Institutions

The global music industry revolves around, and is supported by a number of international organizations, institutions and networks. These range from intellectual property rights and copyright organizations, to trade associations, international broadcasters and music distributors, international conferences and trade shows, to international treaties and conventions. As a general rule, the global nature of the business of music, and in the case of Jamaican music, the very significant level of global penetration and popularity achieved, dictate that special attention be placed on interaction with international institutions and networks. Jamaica's interaction with international entities ranges from fairly effective, to poor.

As far as intellectual property rights and copyrights are concerned, the World Intellectual Property Organization (WIPO) is regarded as the single most important international institution. WIPO is a self-funded agency of the United Nations established in 1967. Its mission is to lead the development of a balanced and effective international intellectual property (IP) system that enables innovation and creativity for the benefit of all. WIPO helps governments, businesses, and society to realize the benefits of IP by providing the following:

- a policy forum to shape balanced international IP rules for a changing world;
- global services to protect IP across borders and to resolve disputes;
- technical infrastructure to connect IP systems and share knowledge;
- cooperation and capacity building programs to enable all countries to use IP for economic, social and cultural development.
- a world reference source for IP information.[92]

Jamaica has maintained a very good working relationship with WIPO over the years, and has secured benefits in training, regulatory reform and institutional strengthening that have had positive impact on the local music industry. The passage of a new Copyright Act in 1993, the establishment of the Jamaica Intellectual Property Office (JIPO) in 2001, the formation of national music collective rights management organizations such as JACAP and JAMMS, and the execution of WIPO funded research on the Jamaican copyright and music industries, are some examples of the organization's positive impact.[93]

The International Federation of the Phonographic Industry (IFPI) and the International Confederation of Societies of Authors and Composers (CISAC), are globally recognized as the international bodies that govern and set operating guidelines for recording industry associa-

---

92. http://www.wipo.int/about-wipo/en/#whatwedo

93. http://www.wipo.int/export/sites/www/copyright/en/performance/pdf/econ_contribution_cr_ja.pdf

tions and music collective management organizations around the world. The IFPI is the global voice of the recording industry. It is a not-for-profit international organization registered in Switzerland in 1933 with offices in London, Brussels, Hong Kong, and Miami, plus a representative office in Beijing. The mission of the IFPI is threefold:

- to promote the value of recorded music, including its economic value in creating growth, jobs, and investment, and its cultural value to society and in people's lives;
- to campaign for the rights of record producers by making sure that the rights of members who create, produce and invest in music are properly protected and enforced;
- to facilitate the expansion of the commercial uses of recorded music by working to help members license and generate commercial value for music through every available channel across the world.

IFPI membership is open to record companies and labels around the world. There are currently over 1300 member companies in over 66 countries. There are no Jamaican companies listed as members of the IFPI. Despite this fact the establishment of the Jamaica Music Society (JAMMS) was facilitated by the IFPI, and the IFPI continues to hold a seat on the board of directors of JAMMS. One of the most important services provided by the IFPI is the publication of annual statistics on the economic performance of the global recording industry, including performance on a per country basis. Jamaican recording industry statistics have never been specifically mentioned in annual IFPI data, and there have never been adequate performance details on Reggae as a music genre. This lack of data could be attributed to the absence of Jamaican/ Reggae record company membership in IFPI.

CISAC is a non-governmental, not-for-profit organization founded in 1926. It is based in France with four regional offices in Burkina Faso, Chile, China and Hungary. As of 2013 CISAC comprised a network of 227 collective management organizations in 120 countries representing the copyright interests of over 3 million music authors, composers and music publishers. CISAC's mission and activities aim to:

1. strengthen and develop its international network of authors' socie-

ties;

2. be the voice of the creators and their collective management organizations (CMOs) on the international scene;

3. adopt and implement quality standards to improve cross-border data exchange amongst authors' societies;

4. support societies' strategic development in every geographic region and artistic repertoire;

5. advocate fostering a legal environment that supports authors' rights on international, regional and national levels

The Jamaica Association of Composers Authors and Publishers (JACAP) was admitted to CISAC membership in 1987.

There are a number of international treaties and conventions that impact global operations in the music industry. Listed below are some of the most important international conventions:

- The Berne Convention for the Protection of Literary and Artistic Works – First implemented in 1886, with various revisions up to and including changes made in 1971
- The Convention for the Protection of Performers, Producers of Phonograms and Broadcasting Organizations ("the Rome Convention") – Agreed on in 1961
- Convention for the Protection of Producers of Phonograms Against Unauthorized Duplication of Their Phonograms – Adopted in 1971
- The Madrid Agreement Concerning the International Registration of Marks (Trade and Service Marks) – adopted in 1889, and the Protocol Relating to the Madrid Agreement – adopted in 1989 and made operational in 1996.
- The Trademark Law Treaty (TLT) – adopted in 1994
- The WIPO Copyright Treaty (WCT) and the WIPO Performances and Phonograms Treaty – Adopted in 1996
- The Singapore Treaty on the Law of Trademarks – Adopted in 2006

Between the years 1993 and 2006 Jamaica took the necessary steps to become a member of all the above treaties except the treaties dealing with trademarks. This represents a clear commitment to the improvement of the regulatory framework for copyright administration, and has contributed to an increased level of awareness and interest among music practitioners and members of the public. Despite this, ignorance regarding copyrights and the value of copyrights remain at an unacceptably low level. Jamaica's failure to become a member of the international trademark treaties has placed local business operators in the music industry at a disadvantage in terms of international registrations to protect the logos and brands they create in association with their products and services.

From a strict legal and business perspective, the Jamaican music industry appears to be sometimes out of synch with accepted practices in the more developed industries of major music markets such as the USA, Japan, UK, Germany, France, Australia, and Canada. There have been attempts at awareness building, exposure and global networking through Jamaican participation at international music trade conferences such as MIDEM, but more frequent and diverse international interaction is required at these and other similar events.

The links and working relationships between Jamaican music associations and their international counterparts have also not been as effective as they should be, as there is need for improved corporate governance and business administration capacity at the local level. Very few local music business operators are aware of, or participate as members of key international networks such as the Music Managers Forum, the International Music Managers Forum, the International Festivals and Events Organization, or the International Federation of Festival Organizations. Jamaica has also not taken full advantage of participation in the annual South By South West Festival and Conferences staged in Austin Texas, which is regarded as the world's largest such event.[94]

An examination of the activities of international music distributors and broadcasters in their presentation and representation of Reggae will reveal a marked difference between the years prior to 2000 and the years since 2000. Prior to 2000 well over twenty Jamaica based recording artists were signed to international recording and music publishing deals with major and large independent labels. Since 2000 this list has diminished significantly, as fewer than five Jamaican artists were signed to international recording and publishing deals at the end of 2014. Similarly, the airtime allocated by international media outlets for the broadcast of

94. https://www.facebook.com/notes/lloyd-stanbury/Reggae-in-austin-the-live-music-capital-of-the-world/10155989728640355

Reggae from Jamaica, has experienced decline from pre-2000 years to post-2000 years.

The lack of professionalism of artists, music producers and artist managers is cited as one of the main reasons for the decline experienced. This breakdown in working relationships between Jamaican Reggae practitioners and their international music distribution and broadcast partners has had a major negative impact on the advancement of the business of Reggae globally. Some international partners have still not recovered from the bad experiences of the past, and have not been able to relate to the new trends and more professional business approach of the emerging group of young roots Reggae artists coming from Jamaica in recent years.

Despite a number of attempts, Reggae is still without an established, scheduled international trade conference or business network. The USA based Reggae Ambassadors Worldwide (RAW), which at its peak attracted global membership in excess of 20,000 is now defunct, after operating since 1996. Between 1999 and 2003, the Caribbean Music Expo conference was successfully staged annually in Ocho Rios, Jamaica, attracting industry participants from over 25 countries. This event has also been on pause.

In June 2014, a Reggae music business panel discussion was presented at the annual Sierra Nevada World Music Festival held in Boonville California. The panel was staged in response to the concerns of performers, music producers, managers, promoters and fans regarding the decline in Reggae music business activity and revenues within the North American music market. As a follow up to the discussions, the Reggae Business Network of North America, (RBN North America), was established as an online network. The RBN is open to Reggae business operators from around the world who strive for professionalism within the music markets of the USA and Canada. It is not a regulatory nor oversight organization, and is designed to provide relevant information and professional development opportunities. A number of subject matter experts in areas such as concert promotions, artist management, publicity, photography, entertainment law and digital and online music promotion and distribution will facilitate the activities of the RBN. [95]

One of the consequences of weak institutional infrastructure in

---

95. https://www.facebook.com/Reggaebusinessnetwork

Reggae, is the absence of an internationally recognized professional practice for music awards that celebrate and recognize creative excellence and/or commercial accomplishments. This deficiency is highlighted each year in the public debates that have now become common whenever the nominees for "Best Reggae Album" are announced for the GRAMMY Awards. The Grammys are the most recognized music awards in the international music industry, and voting participation is limited to members of the Recording Academy established to oversee the Grammy awards process. Unfortunately many Jamaican and other small independent Reggae producers and artists do not seek membership to the Recording Academy, and therefore have very little say in the outcome of these awards. As previously mentioned, the Reggae Academy was established in Jamaica by the Recording Industry Association of Jamaica with membership open to Reggae practitioners and media from around the world. The first Reggae Academy awards were presented in Kingston in February 2008, but there has been no other presentation of the Reggae Academy Awards since then.

Music Awards and Reggae
– Facebook note – January 18, 2015 [96]

As usual the announcement of the nominees for the Reggae category of the GRAMMYS has caused the now familiar flurry of comments from members of the Reggae community and entertainment media. The nominees for the 2014 Best Reggae Album category of the GRAMMYS are: "Fly Rasta" by Ziggy Marley, "Full Frequency" by Sean Paul, "Back on the Controls" by Lee "Scratch" Perry, "The Reggae Power" by Sly and Robbie & Spicy Chocolate, "Out of Many, One Music" by Shaggy, and "Amid the Noise and Haste" by SOJA. Already we have seen media reports and comments making mention of projects being omitted, as well as various opinions expressed regarding the GRAMMYS. One thing is for certain, the GRAMMYS attract more attention and comments than any other music award, and despite the criticisms, it is clear that a GRAMMY win or nomination does mean something to artists.

Music awards are a very important aspect of the international

---

96. https://www.facebook.com/notes/lloyd-stanbury/music-awards-and-Reggae/101556320733
30355?pnref=lhc

music industry. It is therefore necessary for performers, composers and producers of music, and the media and management representatives who support their recordings, to inform themselves and get involved in the music awards process. A full understanding of the procedures by which entries are submitted, nominations decided and winners selected, is essential. Without knowledge and active participation you will continue to be on the fringe, either shouting from the galleries or making disgruntled comments.

So, how does the GRAMMYS work? I would strongly recommend that readers of this article take a look at the web site for the Recording Academy, which is the entity that determines how entries are submitted, and nominees and winners chosen. What is clear with the GRAMMYS is that performers, producers, songwriters, managers and label executives need to become members of the Academy to be able to have a say, and to influence the process of selecting winners. You are not required to be a citizen of the USA to become a member of the Academy.

As far as the Jamaican and global Reggae music industry is concerned, I think we need to come together to establish our own internationally recognized music awards that cater specifically to the Reggae music genre, in much the same way as Hip Hop, Country, Latin and other genres have done.

There are many models out there for music awards. Some awards are developed by media entities such as MTV, Billboard and BET, and winners are determined by popularity through public voting participation. The GRAMMYS are based on voting by persons from within the recording industry, and is not based on chart success or record sales.

There have been a number of awards that cater in varying degrees to the Jamaican and Reggae music community. With the exception of the honour awards presented annually by Jamaica Reggae Industry Association/JaRIA, no such award exists currently inside Jamaica. The JaRIA Honour Awards are presented in February each year and recognizes the lifetime achievement of persons involved in Reggae. It is not about current or recent releases or performances. On the international level there is the Ephraim Martin promoted International Reggae and World Music Awards/IRAWMA originating out of Chicago. As the name suggests IRAWMA caters to Reggae, Soca and World Beat music. It is not specific to Reggae.

In 2008 the Recording Industry Association of Jamaica took a bold step in establishing the Reggae Academy, with a view to developing an international music award specifically dedicated to Reggae and Dancehall. The Reggae Academy was designed based on the Recording Academy/GRAMMY model with membership open to vocalists, songwriters, music producers, recording engineers, music video producers, agents, label executives, managers and media representatives from around the world involved in the Reggae recording business. The Reggae Academy Awards were successfully staged in February 2008 in Kingston. Its presentation also facilitated the declaration of the month of February as Reggae Month by then Jamaican Prime Minister Bruce Golding, and Governor General Sir Kenneth Hall.

The Reggae Academy Awards 2008 was hailed by many as the best music award show ever presented for Reggae. Inadequate sponsorship support and disagreements between key individuals within the Academy administration and the wider Jamaican Reggae community, have caused the Reggae Academy Awards to be placed on pause. As long as Reggae artists, music producers, labels, managers and media representatives remain unwilling to unite and cooperate in establishing their own international awards, and as long as they remain non-members of the GRAMMY Academy, then they should stop talking and accept what they get.

The Caribbean Music Industry
– Facebook note – Sunday, February 21, 2010 [97]

There has been quite a bit of talk over the past few years about the need to grow and better structure the Caribbean music industry. While open discussions and lobbying is a necessary part of the development process, it is my view that way too much emphasis has been placed on talk, meetings and fact finding overseas missions, while the positive actions being taken by qualified industry experts tend to either go un-noticed, or are the subject of criticism.

---

97. https://www.facebook.com/notes/lloyd-stanbury/the-caribbean-music-industry/10150091611315355

In my view the work being done by the only legitimate Caribbean regional music industry entity Caribbean Copyright Link (CCL) is a perfect demonstration of my point. The CCL was formed to represent the collective global copyright and neighbouring rights interests of national societies serving Caribbean songwriters, music publishers, producers, and performers. The CCL membership includes the Jamaica Association of Composers, Authors and Publishers (JACAP), the Jamaica Music Society (JAMMS), the Copyright Collection Organization of Trinidad and Tobago (COTT), the Copyright Society of Composers, Authors and Publishers (COSCAP) in Barbados, and the Eastern Caribbean Copyright Organization (ECCO). The CCL has for many years been working very closely with international intellectual property rights organizations such as the World Intellectual Property Organization (WIPO), the International Federation of the Phonographic Industry (IFPI) and the International Confederation of Authors and Composers Societies (CISAC).

The CCL has worked tirelessly in recent years in an effort to improve regional and global conditions for rights administration and royalty collection, and has also been providing statistics with regard to the trends in national and regional music royalty collections. I do recall receiving information circulated by the CCL a few years back pointing to the negative trends in regional royalty collections and the disparity between royalty inflows and outflows as between the Caribbean and the rest of the world.

The CCL must also be commended for its very active role in seeking to identify and acquire appropriate technology for the use of its member organizations in the music use monitoring process. Members of the CCL executive have also been actively participating in relevant research and workshop training for the benefit of music rights holders and users in the region.

The businesses of music, entertainment, and the cultural industries in general have now become fashionable in the Caribbean. This has resulted in the birth and announcement of a number of new private regional initiatives that purport to deal with the structured development of the businesses of music and entertainment at the regional level. While these private initiatives are welcomed and should definitely be encouraged, it is also necessary that we recognize and work with existing regional expertise, such as that developed through the work being done by the CCL.

The business of music is still about the commercial exploitation of various aspects of intellectual property rights, as well as the rendering of performance and production services. It is therefore absolutely necessary that these new initiatives are guided by the lessons learned and experience gained by entities such as the CCL and others that have a proven track record in intellectual property rights administration and related performance and production services arrangements.

I was inspired to write this note after reading two reports in Jamaican daily newspapers about trends in the global music trade as these relate to Jamaican and Caribbean music. You may also find these newspaper reports interesting:[98] [99]

Summary

- Music associations should be strengthened by increasing membership participation and improving the quality of their administration through training and engagement of more qualified managers.
- An increased level of awareness is required by industry operators regarding the requirements and conventional practices of the business of music so as to reduce mistrust.
- The issue of Payola needs to be tackled with a view to restricting its impact.
- International institutional relationships must be improved.
- A greater level of understanding of the role and importance of international music institutions is required.
- There is need for a greater and more diverse level of participation in international music trade events.
- Training is required to instill professionalism in artists, producers and managers.

---

98. http://www.jamaicaobserver.com/entertainment/Music-royalties-feb-21
99. http://jamaica-gleaner.com/gleaner/20100221/ent/ent1.html

Legalize It – Understanding Copyrights and Contracts

The business of music has its economic foundation in the under-standing, appreciation, and application of principles of law that arise from legislation and/or the common law practices in the law of contracts. The average recording artist, music producer and show promoter will of necessity encounter a variety of contractual relation-ships and legislative provisions in the ordinary course of business, and to an extent much greater than most other areas of commercial activity. Failure to appropriately prepare and deal with the various legal issues of the business of music is without question, preparing to fail.

A Jamaican Legacy of Informality and Ignorance

In my over thirty years of practice as an entertainment attorney and music business consultant, I have made two significant and instructive observations. These are:

1. the regularity with which I am approached by Jamaican recording artists and songwriters with claims that they have participated in re-cording projects for which they have either received no compensa-tion or inadequate compensation;

2. the regularity with which internationally successful original Jamai-can musical compositions result in songwriter disputes and law suits.

Both situations mentioned above exemplify a long-standing prob-lem that has plagued Jamaican music business for well over 50 years.

Jamaican industry practitioners have failed to recognize and deal with the fact that the business of music is built upon a foundation of respect for and understanding of the significance of intellectual property law and the law of contracts. For the most part, Jamaican music is produced in a very informal environment where artists and music producers get together and often record without any discussions or arrangements regarding product ownership, rights or royalties. Written recording agreements between music producers and recording artists are rarely entered into, and in those cases where agreements are signed, artists are mostly unaware of the implications of what they signed. There are rarely any written agreements between artists and the persons they work with as their managers.

Prior to the enactment of the Jamaican Copyright Act in 1993 there was the widely held belief that copyright law did not exist in Jamaica, despite the fact that the old UK Copyright Act of 1911 was still applicable. Consequently, with the exception of the activities of the local branch of the UK based Performing Rights Society (PRS), which represented the interests of songwriters, very little information was provided to musicians regarding issues to do with music authorship, composition, and music publishing. For example, the vast majority of Jamaican artists were not aware of the music composition rights of studio musicians who created original music while performing on recording sessions. Very little information existed with regard to the rights of songwriters to earn from sales of recordings that included their musical compositions. A lingering anomaly from this lack of knowledge about songwriters' rights to royalties from record sales is the fact that Jamaica is still without a national collective management organization to deal with mechanical royalty collections.

The environment of informality and ignorance that exists in Jamaican music production inevitably results in many disputes between recording artists, studio musicians, music producers, and songwriters. There have been numerous stories about royalty   rip-offs and unfair business deals which have fueled a high level of mistrust within the local industry. Until the enactment in 1993 of the Jamaican Copyright Act, and the subsequent establishment of institutions such as the Jamaica Association of Composers Authors and Publisher (JACAP), the Jamaica Music Society (JAMMS), and the Jamaica Intellectual Property Office (JIPO), there were no support mechanisms for awareness building with regard to copyrights and the business of music.

The attitudes of many Reggae artists towards documentation, contracts and laws related to their music activities has been strongly influenced by the resistance of Rastafari to the Babylon system of colonial laws and methods, such as written contracts for business. Many Rasta Reggae artists regard their role in music as a mission to carry out JAH's works, as against a strict business endeavour. Much of 1960s and 70s Reggae music formed the message and soundtrack of an African liberation and Rastafari resistance movement against colonialism. For many artists, the making of music was and still is regarded as a spiritual and socio-political mission as against a business activity. The signing of written contracts is an exercise often shunned by these artists, usually to their eventual economic detriment. The lack of trust and low levels of appreciation for legal and contractual issues in music is also manifested in the resistance of many Jamaican artists to the idea of collective representation through membership in relevant music associations.

Law and the Business of Music in Jamaica

The business of music is a complex arena of activities that impact the rights of various participants who function at the creative, technical, administrative or representational levels. It is therefore necessary for industry participants to surround themselves with advisors with the requisite knowledge and experience to guide them through. In order to function effectively, industry practitioners should also seek to acquire a minimum basic level of understanding of the legal issues involved in doing business, including consideration of the following:

1. the type of business entity to use – sole proprietorship, partnership, or registered company;
2. the protection of logos, trademarks and domain names;
3. the negotiation and management of contracts for recording and distribution;
4. the negotiation and management of contracts for live performance services and the staging of events;
5. the management of music copyrights and related rights;
6. arrangements between the artist and his/her managers and representatives;
7. local and international taxation and other government regulations.

The vast majority of music business operators in Jamaica are individuals who function either solely, or in informal partnerships with others. This includes creative practitioners such as songwriters, music producers, audio-visual producers, visual artists, vocalists and musicians, as well as technical and administrative service providers. There is no precise data available with regard to the number of practicing vocalists, songwriters, musicians, music producers. Nor is there accurate data on the number of technical and administrative service providers there are operating in the Jamaican music industry.

The Jamaica Association of Composers Authors and Publishers (JACAP) declares its Jamaican membership at over 3,400 songwriters and music publishers, while the Jamaica Music Society (JAMMS) declares its local membership at over 600 music producers. The longest serving membership organization for music in Jamaica is the musicians union Jamaica Federation of Musicians (JFM) which was formed in 1958. The JFM has been affiliated with the International Federation of Musicians for several years. Since its formation the JFM has attracted membership from thousands of Jamaica musicians, vocal performers and dancers, but annual dues paying membership has been low. The organization has however been the most consistent source of information and advocacy on behalf of local music industry development for several decades. In 2014 the Jamaican Ministry of Tourism and Entertainment announced the implementation of a registration system for the entertainment industry. There is however some resistance to this initiative as the criteria for registration requires more detail and clarity.

Despite the relatively large number of music and entertainment business practitioners in Jamaica, and the necessity for specialized legal services to address various issues, the practice of entertainment law has not been sufficiently developed. Very few Jamaican attorneys have acquired the requisite skills and experience to service the music and entertainment sector. At the same time, the majority of entertainment industry practitioners operate informally without paying adequate attention to the legal issues of contracts and the protection of intellectual property rights.

The "Rip-off" Syndrome in Jamaican Music

Anyone who has been around the Jamaican music business for a while will be sure to encounter the constant complaint by artists, about being robbed of their rights and cheated out of royalties from the commercial exploitation of their musical compositions and sound recordings. My experience has been that some of these stories are in fact true, as many persons have been taken advantage of by the parties with whom they do business. On the other hand, there are also many instances where, through ignorance and lack of appropriate representation, artists fail to take necessary precautions to secure their rights, and are often mistaken about their market value and how much their music sells.

The economic benefits that flow from music creation and public consumption are founded on principles of copyright and intellectual property law, as well as the law of contracts. To effectively analyze what is referred to in this section as the "Rip-Off" Syndrome within the Jamaican music industry, it is therefore necessary to examine and clarify some of the basics of Copyright Law as it relates to the business of music.

For every sound recording produced there are basically three categories of creative rights holders that are recognized and protected by law. These are:

- the songwriters – who are responsible for creating the original music and lyrics that comprise what is referred to in music and copyright terminology as the musical composition, or song, as we commonly call it;
- the music producer – who is responsible for the creation and ownership of a sound recording or master of a musical composition;
- the performers – who are the vocalists and musicians who perform in studio at a recording session.

Jamaica's Copyright Act works in tandem with Copyright laws in many other countries, as Jamaica is party to international treaties covering musical compositions and sound recordings, where rights are protected internationally. These rights include, but are not limited to the following:
- the right of composers and authors of musical compositions to compensation from the sales of recordings that include their original compositions.

- the right of composers and authors of musical compositions to be compensated from the public performance and broadcast of their works by traditional and new digital and online means.
- the right of authors and composers of musical works to be credited, and to object to modifications of their works.
- the right of music producers to be compensated from public performance and broadcast of their sound recordings on radio, TV, and by digital transmissions.
- the right of performers on sound recordings (vocalists and musicians) to be compensated from the public performance and broadcast of sound recordings that include their performance.

A significant amount of the complaints, disputes and allegations about "rip off" in the Jamaican music industry relate to the issue of songwriters' credits, and the splits between collaborators regarding ownership and share of royalties and other income. The complaints, disputes and allegations have been mainly due to lack of understanding among songwriters, music producers and recording artists about the copyright implications of their music collaborations. Since the enactment of the Jamaican Copyright Act in 1993 and the establishment of institutions such as the Jamaica Intellectual Property Office, the Jamaica Association of Composers Authors and Publishers, and the Jamaica Music Society, there has been a significant increase in the level of awareness among artists regarding the implications of copyrights on the business of music. This has resulted in more attention being placed on the importance of sorting out credits and splits between persons who collaborate in the creation of musical compositions and the production of related sound recordings.

Despite increased awareness in recent years, the importance of copyright law and rights management as the foundation for economic benefits in the recording industry is still underplayed in Jamaica. The country is still without a collective management organization that is dedicated to the monitoring and collection of songwriters' royalties (mechanical royalties) due from record sales. There is also no functioning national collective management organization in Jamaica to represent the rights of performers (vocalists and musicians) regarding royalties due for public performances and broadcasts of the sound recordings in which they participate.

Music Rights Administration in Jamaica

Copyright law confers on songwriters, music producers and performers, certain exclusive rights related to the sale, public performance and broadcast of musical compositions and sound recordings that incorporate their creative and other inputs. In order to represent these exclusive rights on a collective basis, the law also recognizes and enables the establishments of licensing schemes that allow for the operation of what is commonly referred to in the industry as Collective Management Organizations, CMOs or collecting societies. Collecting societies act on behalf of their members (authors, composers, performers and music producers), and issue licenses to users authorizing the use of the works of their members. Collecting societies negotiate the rates and other license terms applicable to users on behalf of their membership, and collect and distribute royalty payments to members.

At present the Jamaican Copyright Act does not enable the establishment of licensing schemes for the administration of the rights of performers. This deficiency in the Jamaican law has prevented the formal establishment of a collecting society to act on behalf of performers, a situation that has been to the disadvantage of Jamaican music performers, and prevented collections of millions of US dollars in performers royalties generated from international public performance uses in several countries. There has been a number of media reports highlighting the fact that significant sums of money remain unpaid to Jamaican performers for public performance royalties from users in countries such as France.

The Jamaica Association of Authors Composers and Publishers (JACAP) and the Jamaica Music Society (JAMMS) currently operate collective management organizations for the Jamaican music industry, providing representation for several thousand Jamaican authors, composers and music producers. Both JACAP and JAMMS have international affiliations and reciprocal agreements that enable them to represent Jamaican music repertoire globally. Both organizations are, however, in need of further development at the internal administrative level, with more effective monitoring of the use of Jamaican music repertoire. Revenues generated from broadcast and other public performance use of Jamaican music repertoire in foreign countries do not accurately reflect the global popularity of Jamaican musical compositions and sound recordings.

166

To Sign or Not to Sign – Contracts and Music Business in Jamaica

The nature of the business of music is such that at some stage, all practicing recording artists, performers, songwriters and music producers will of necessity enter into relationships that require contractual considerations. These relationships range from artist/producer collaborations, or being booked to play at a club or festival, to representation arrangements with managers, agents, music publishers or record distributors.

The successful execution of the production, presentation and distribution of music products and services require a series of collaborative partnerships between creators, performers, technical suppliers and management representatives. While some of these relationships are governed by domestic and international copyright systems, many also rely on the negotiation and execution of contracts between the collaborating partners. As is the case with the business of copyrights, the majority of practitioners in the Jamaican music industry have operated informally, and with much ignorance about entertainment contracts. Experience has shown that many of the allegations of "rip off" and bad business relationships are the result of the failure to negotiate and put in place appropriate written agreements.

The types of relationships and contracts required for operation of a professional music enterprise are many and varied. Proper treatment of the business of music contracts would therefore require a book in itself. In this chapter of REGGAE ROADBLOCKS we highlight some of the more frequently encountered relationships and agreements. We also discuss the challenges and misunderstandings normally associated with these relationships.

Artist and Manager Agreement

The relationship between an artist and his/her manager is one of the most important relationships in the development of a professional music business operation. Good artist management sets the stage for the establishment and maintenance of effective working relationships between an artist and other necessary partners in the processes of music production, distribution, promotion and presentation. It is the responsibility of the artist manager to provide the career development guidance and counsel

167

required by every artist, and to act as the team leader and coordinator of the activities of all other artist representatives.

To be effective an artist manager should ensure he or she has a working knowledge of the legal and business development aspects of the music industry, at both the national and global levels. Typically this knowledge is gained from mentorship, work experience, research and training, or through the guidance of an expert consultant and advisor. Good artist managers are also required to have effective oral and written communication skills, and the ability to handle interpersonal relationships in a fast paced work environment to ensure punctuality and responsiveness.

The role of the artist manager is frequently misunderstood by industry practitioners. There is also the tendency of artists to either try to manage themselves, or to engage family members and trusted friends as their managers. In many instances these family member or friend managers do not possess the required knowledge, experience or skills to adequately represent the artist, and refuse to engage appropriate experienced advisors. There are numerous instances of bad deals, inappropriate actions and unprofessionalism within the local and international Reggae music community as a consequence of bad artist management. Bad artist management and lack of artist management have been major barriers to the development of the Jamaican music industry. A major shift in approach is required towards a more informed environment where management contracts are properly negotiated and administered.

Several important issues should be considered in the process of negotiating, executing, and administering an artist management contract. Included among these are the following:

Purpose of the Agreement – The overall objective of artist management is to provide career guidance and counseling towards the production, packaging and presentation of creative products and services. Management also plays an important role in the building of awareness and demand for an artist's products and services. The artist management agreement provides the framework for the manager to function as team leader in the coordination of the activities of all other representatives of the artist.

Personal and Business Manager – Artist management in music is time consuming and covers a range of developmental activities. Management may also include similar duties to those normally provided by publicity agents, booking agents and business managers. Artist personal managers typically assume responsibility for general career development and the coordination of all related activities. A business manager typically focuses on legal, taxation and other financial and accounting issues. Business managers are often attorneys or certified public accountants. In many instances the functions of personal and business manager are incorporated in one and provided by the same individual.

Duration of the Management Relationship – In negotiating a management agreement serious consideration should be given to the timeframe within which the management services are to be provided. The agreement should clearly stipulate start date and end date, and the conditions for termination and/or extension. In the case of new and emerging artists, it is of critical importance that both parties take into consideration the time required for development of an artist's career, including creating, packaging, presenting and building awareness to the point where music products and services are in demand. The initial duration of artist management contracts normally ranges between one and five years, with options for renewal.

Compensation of Manager and Other Financial Considerations – Artist management contracts unusually provide for compensation to the manager in the form of a commission on the gross earnings from all sources in the entertainment industry. This commission ranges from a low of 15 percent to a high of 25 percent. In some special circumstances the manager's compensation commission may be even higher, or be restricted to income generated only from certain agreed activities. This restricted approach to commissioning income is however not the recommended or usual approach, as it fails to take into consideration the connected implications of various activities required in artist management. For example, time spent by a manager on building awareness does affect the songwriting and music publishing earnings of an artist, even though an artist may operate his or her own publishing company or have a separate publishing agreement with a third party. Artist managers often expend their own funds on the developmental activities of the artists they work with. Appropriate provisions should be incorporated in a management contract to address the issue of reimbursement to the manager for expenses incurred on behalf of the artist.

Exclusivity – Artist management contracts usually provide that the artist will contract just one person, or a group of persons acting in partnership or as a registered corporation, to provide management services. In other words services are provided exclusively by one manager or group of managers. On the other hand managers are free to enter into management agreements with more than one artist at the same time.

Power of Attorney – One of the key functions of an artist manager is the negotiation and execution of contracts on behalf of the artist represented. In order to legally perform this function it is necessary that the artist management contract includes the grant of a power of attorney to the manager with authority to execute contracts. The extent of this authority can vary from case to case.

Scope of the Relationship – Artist management agreements are usually designed to cover all activities of the artist in the entertainment industry worldwide. There are however instances where certain entertainment activities undertaken by the artist are excluded from the scope of the manager's responsibilities. One very common example in the Jamaican music industry is the exclusion of management from the activity of making and delivering "specials" or "dub-plates" for sound systems. Some artists have also been known to exclude management from involvement in songwriting and music publishing activities and earnings.

Recording Artist and Music Producer

Jamaica has had a long history as a prolific producer of sound recordings. In a February 4, 1995 Billboard report on the Jamaican Reggae industry, "Music Thrives as Studios Proliferate", Elena Oumano cited "industry observers" stating that Jamaica was the highest producer of sound recordings in the world per capita. Jamaica also has possibly the highest number of commercial and personal recording studios per capita in the world. A very large percentage of the Jamaican youth population have demonstrated interest in recording and performing music, and with the advent of digital and computerized music production technology, almost every youth in Jamaica with access to a computer now has the ability to become a music producer of sorts.

As noted before, the Jamaican music industry developed in an environment where copyright law, the business of contracts and rights protection were not adequately understood. While there has been some increase in the level of awareness about copyright law and the importance of contracts, the vast majority of recording artists and music producers still collaborate in recording, producing and distributing sound recordings to the   public without entering into formal arrangements.

The relationship between a recording artist and a music producer creates the foundation for the music recording industry. It is the basis upon which arrangements are made for the commercial exploitation of sound recordings. When a recording artist and music producer get together to work in a recording studio, a collaborative business partnership is created that affects the rights to the proceeds from the sale and other commercial use of the recordings they produce. In order to avoid issues about rights and entitlements, it is therefore imperative that recording artists and music producers discuss and arrive at mutually acceptable arrangements for every sound recording that they work on together. These arrangements can easily be documented in simple artist producer contracts, or in more comprehensive artist recording and development contracts. Unfortunately, within the Jamaican recording industry the vast majority of recording artists and music producers have failed to put in place appropriate business arrangements for the recordings they make. This has hampered the smooth flow of Jamaican recorded music into the legitimate global commercial music space, as a result of the frequent recording artist and music producer disputes that occur.

A quote from Wailers bassist, Aston "Family Man" Barrett in a February 1995 Billboard newspaper interview is instructive: "...To spread a message of roots culture and reality (is) a strong force of course. But I'm getting to learn that in business, you do not get what you deserve, only what you negotiate."

Key Contractual Issues

The following are some of the key issues to be considered in the recording artist music producer contractual relationship:

The parties to a Music Recording Agreement – The parties to a recording contract are the recording artist on the one hand and the music producer or record label on the other.

The Main Purpose of the Agreement – Recording agreements between artist and producer or artist and record label serve the purpose of establishing the respective rights and entitlements of each party that will flow from the commercial exploitation of a sound recording.

Types of recording contracts – There are various types of record-ing contracts that an artist may enter into with a producer or record label. These range from a basic agreement for the recording of one specific song, to an agreement for the recording of several songs or an album, and exclusive recording and artist development contracts that run for a prescribed period of time. Many exclusive long term recording and artist development contracts today also incorporate provisions enabling inves-tor/producers to participate in "non-record" income, such as earnings from live shows, branding, and endorsements.

Responsibilities of the music producer or label – The music producer or label has the primary responsibility for the coordination of creative production inputs of a studio recording session which often includes the funding of recording expenses. The producer or label is also required to ensure that all appropriate music production and songwrit-ing credits are documented to protect the rights of all participants in the production process. The above issues should be considered and appro-priately addressed in contractual arrangements between an artist and his music producer or record label.

Regarding the treatment of production expenses: it is the accepted procedure in the recording industry that music production expenses, in-cluding studio expenses, mastering expenses and packaging and design expenses incurred by a music producer or record label, are properly doc-umented and recouped from record sales income prior to the sharing of profits from commercial exploitation of the sound recording. Recording agreements should also address these issues.

Ownership of Sound Recording Master – A recording agreement should ensure that the ownership of sound recording masters is clearly outlined. The norm is that the person or entity that funds the recording process will have exclusive rights to ownership of the resulting masters. The music producer or label is usually the person or entity that funds the recording process, and is therefore typically identified as the owner of the sound recording master. Where a recording artist also contributes to the funding of recording expenses the parties should arrive at a clear understanding as to how the artist's funding input will be treated, and make a decision on whether or not sound recording master ownership will be shared between the artist and producer or label.

Royalties and Income Splits – A recording contract must also address the issue of the sharing of record sales proceeds between the artist and producer or label. The share of recording sales income due to each party is normally determined in the music industry by providing for artist royalties and producer royalties as a percentage of retail price of recordings sold. The compensation of artists and producers from sound recording exploitation may also be based on percentage splits of the net proceeds of sale and other income generated.

Treatment of Original Musical Compositions – The interest of the copyright owners in original musical compositions that are recorded by an artist and producer or label is also of critical importance. A properly constructed recording contract should include a songwriter split section that outlines the percentages due to each person that makes a creative contribution to writing lyrics and composing the music accompanying the lyrics recorded.

Performer and Show Promoter

Live performances and the promotion of concerts and music festivals have always been the most vibrant part of the Jamaican music industry, both locally and internationally. This area has also had the greatest level of written documentation and contractual activity, and is likely the area with the highest level of knowledge and awareness among Jamaican industry practitioners. Despite this, there are still many instances of disputes between live performing artists and show promoters.

There are frequent instances of failure by artists and promoters to adhere strictly to the conditions of the contracts into which they enter. These complaints range from the refusal of artists to appear and perform as contracted, to the refusal of promoters to honor their obligations related to the provision of specified equipment and services, and even the payment of fees. Many Jamaican artists are still in the habit of opting out of prior contracted performance engagements as they chase more lucrative subsequent offers.

The typical live performance contract is made either between the performing artist and the promoter of the show, or a booking agent acting on behalf of the artist, and the show promoter. The contracts usually address issues such as performance fees, (normally payable by 50 percent upon signing and 50 percent on the day of the show before performance), duration of performance, performance time, and artist hospitality and merchandising issues. International performance contracts also address transportation, accommodation and compliance with local laws pertaining to work permits and taxation. The most performance contracts negotiated by Jamaican performers and show promoters do not adequately address rights issues related to audio and video recordings and photography at shows. As a consequence there is much confusion and mis-understanding with regard to who has the right to record or capture images, and what is legally permitted where sound and images are recorded at live events.

Music Producer/Record Label and Music Distributors/ Licensees

The global recording industry has been going through major changes over the past ten years, primarily because of adjustments in consumption patterns and the impact of new digital and Internet technology on recorded music sales. After reporting reduced income from recorded music sales for several years, the global recorded music sales report of the IFPI finally showed sales increases in 2012, and a virtual standstill in sales growth for 2013. Although most music genres experienced declines in sales of physical products in the first decade of the 21st century, they have also experienced exponential income growth from legitimate digital music sales and streaming. It is however interesting to note that recorded Jamaican Reggae music has experienced sales declines in recent years at rates that are significantly greater than all other music genres. The jury is still out on the reasons recorded Jamaican Reggae music has had this very poor and troubling performance in recent years.

Despite the shifts taking place and the emergence of new recorded music sales models that place more emphasis on a "do it yourself" approach, it is still necessary for music producers and labels to address contractual issues related to music distribution by third party distributors and licensees. The relevance of traditional major and independent labels and distributors has declined somewhat, as new digital and Internet technology based entities have emerged as music distributors. Music distribution contracts have now been varied to account for the emerging technologically driven digital distribution channels.

In addressing recorded music distribution and licensing contracts one still needs to consider the following:

Purpose of the Agreement – Is the agreement structured to provide mere warehousing and retail services, or is there an obligation on the part of the distributor/licensee to provide promotional support, and if so, to what extent?

Different Types of Distribution Agreements – Is the distribution agreement exclusive or non-exclusive to the distributor, and is it confined to a specific country or region, or is it global. Is the distribution agreement for a single product or for a defined group of products owned and controlled by the producer or label?

Master Use Rights – Does the distribution/licensing agreement confer master ownership rights to the distribution company, or does it merely grant rights to distribute for a specified period?

Financial Considerations – Does the agreement include payment to producer or label by the distributor/licensee of an advance against royalties or share of the income due to producer, and what is the agreed royalty rate or share of income from sales?

Sub-Licensing by Distributor – Does the agreement permit sub-licensing to third parties by the distributor, and are royalty or income share reductions and deductions allowed?

Songwriters and Music Publishers

The activity of songwriting and music publishing is one of the most important and lucrative aspects of the business of music. Unfortunately, in the Jamaican music industry songwriting and music publishing activities also happen to be the least understood. Many Jamaican songwriters and their managers do not know the difference between mechanical rights and resulting royalties due from music sales, and public performance rights and royalties due from airplay and other public presentations of music. The distinction between collection societies and music publishing companies is also not clearly understood by many in the Jamaican music industry, and there is also much confusion as to what creative inputs entitle someone to be credited as a songwriter.

Disputes between studio musicians who make original creative inputs as composers and the recording artists and music producers they work with are the order of the day in the Jamaican music industry. There is very little understanding with regard to the copyright law principles governing the use and adaptation of existing original musical compositions. These weaknesses contribute to the loss and/or misappropriation of songwriting income due to a large number of Jamaican artists.

Songwriters' Splits Agreements – In the global copyright law and music publishing arena songwriters are regarded as the persons who make original creative contributions to the composition of music or the authorship of words incorporated in a song. Recording artists, studio musicians and music producers should ensure that the inputs of the songwriting participants for each original composition that they collaborate on, is represented in writing with a simple split sheet. The songwriters' split sheet should include the names of all contributing music composers and all contributing authors of lyrics with agreed percentages of copyright ownership clearly stated beside each name.

Music Publishing Contracts – The management of the songwriting rights of music composers and authors is handled in the music industry by music publishing companies. Typically a music publisher signs a songwriter or music publishing contract with original songwriters by virtue of which the publisher is given the right and authority to act on behalf of the songwriter. Music publishing contracts vary from publishing administration agreements which do not transfer any copyright interest to the publisher, to publishing agreements that assign copyright interest to the publisher for anywhere between a fixed number of years, and the lifetime of the copyrights in the songs covered in the agreement.

Publishing Administration Contracts – A typical publishing administration contract would be for a specific number of years, ranging anywhere from 1 to 3, wherein the publisher earns a commission of 10 percent – 15 percent for taking care of the administrative work required to register songs with collection societies and the sourcing of income generating commercial uses for the songs administered. No interest in the ownership of copyrights in the songs administered is assigned in administration deals.

Publishing Contract for Specified Number of Songs – A music publishing agreement can be executed in relation to one song or a specific list of songs owned and/or controlled fully or partly by a songwriter. Such an agreement will usually assign to the publisher an agreed upon percentage interest in the copyrights owned by the songwriter for either a specific period of time or for the lifetime of the copyright in the songs covered by the contract. It is not uncommon for publishing contracts to provide for the assignment to the publisher of a 100 percent interest in the ownership of the copyright share of the songwriter for the period of time specified in the contract. Songwriters and publishers are however also known to split copyright ownership in instances where the songwriter also wishes to participate as a co-publisher. A publishing contract usually outlines the percentages in which the publisher and the songwriter will share income generated from recorded music sales, from synchronization licenses for motion picture use, from public performance uses, from cover versions, and from sheet music sold, and other uses.

Exclusive songwriter/publishing contract – An exclusive songwriter or music publishing agreement usually commits the songwriter to assigning all original songs created by the songwriter during the lifetime of the contract. Contract lifetime can vary from 1 to 5 years with option provisions to increase the contract period. All songs created by the songwriter during the initial and renewed option period will automatically fall within the contract. Exclusive songwriters contracts will also include similar provisions as outlined in the preceding paragraph in relation to assignment of copyrights, songwriter music publisher income splits, duration for which rights are assigned to publisher, and co-publishing, if so agreed.

The Band Agreement

Musicians and performers who agree to work together as a band or group should ensure that a band or group agreement is discussed and formalized in writing. It is imperative that every member of the band or group knows what the 'deal' is between the members as a collective. For example if one member owns recording facilities or transportation that is used for the group's business, how will this be treated. The question of ownership of band name and logo must also be addressed. Responsibilities for managing finances and other business responsibilities must be clearly outlined, likewise the treatment of creative inputs such as songwriting and music production. Many bands run into trouble and even fall apart because there is no clear agreement put in place at the start.

New Approaches and New Business Models

As new digital and Internet technologies emerge and evolve, they continue to impact delivery and consumption patterns and trends in the music industry. The traditional business models in the music industry are rapidly changing. The Internet has literally destroyed old record label models of doing business, while at the same time providing new and exciting opportunities for recording artists and music producers to interact directly with their fans, and to distribute and promote music effectively and efficiently on a global scale. Several new music industry players have also emerged in the recording industry including sponsors, live music organizations, investment companies, computer hardware and software companies, and Internet and mobile technology companies. Consequently new variations of the traditional music contracts have become more and more common, and so called "standard" deals are fast becoming a thing of the past.

In recent years Jamaica has experienced an upsurge in the domestic and international popularity of young Roots Reggae artists in a phenomenon that became known as the "Reggae Revival". A number of the prominent artists identified with this movement have been releasing albums independently on their own labels and touring extensively in Europe an North America due mainly to their effective use of social media and digital distribution networks to promote and deliver recordings to their fans globally. "Reggae Revival" artists such as Chronixx, Protoje, Jah9, Raging Fyah, and Kabaka Pyramid have all managed to successfully introduce and present themselves and their music to global audiences without making traditional record distribution deals.

Although technological changes have significantly affected the way music business is done today, legal issues pertaining to copyrights and entertainment contracts remain very relevant, albeit in a new and changing digital environment. Jamaican "Reggae Revival" artists have capitalized on the opportunities for direct promotion and distribution. They do however need to place greater emphasis on securing relevant legal and business advice, guidance and management, to take them further.

The Marley Copyright Case
– Facebook note – September 16, 2010 [100]

Recently there has been widespread reporting on the result of a law suit filed by the Marley family company Fifty-Six Hope Road

---

100. https://www.facebook.com/notes/lloyd-stanbury/the-marley-copyright-case/10150273497860355

Music Limited against Universal Music Group (UMG). According to reports in various international publications, on Friday September 10, 2010 US District Court Judge Denise Cote ruled that the copyrights in the sound recordings of five Marley albums were the property of UMG. The albums in question "Catch a Fire," "Burnin'," "Natty Dread," "Rastaman Vibrations" and "Exodus" were recorded by Marley under his recording agreement with Island Records.

The news about this ruling has resulted in a flurry of blog comments from Marley and Reggae fans around the world, mostly representing an outcry against injustice and greed on the part of the record companies. One of the points made on behalf of the Marley family company in the case was that UMG intentionally withheld royalties from Fifty-Six Hope Road Music Limited. The family apparently claims entitlement to royalty payments to their company on the basis of a 1995 agreement which assigned rights under the recording contracts to Fifty-Six Hope Road Music Limited. From a legal standpoint, the key question is: what rights do the family have under the recording contracts as beneficiaries of the Marley estate?

The law in the USA regarding the concept of "work for hire" is very clear, and it appears from the facts of this case that the recordings in question were all recorded by Marley on a "work for hire" basis by virtue of relevant stipulations in his recording contract. What this means in layman's terms is that the ownership of those recording masters vests 100 percent with the record company. This does not however mean that the recording artist and his estate are not entitled to receive royalties from the commercial exploitation of the recordings. Recording contracts typically stipulate an agreed royalty rate payable by the label to the artist based on a percentage of future record sales in ALL formats now known and to be invented in the future.

The media reports to date on this case are typical of most entertainment reports, where emphasis is placed on sensational headlines rather than relevant facts. The reports do not indicate what the judge's ruling was with regard to the entitlement of the Marley family and Fifty-Six Hope Road Music Limited to the royalties allegedly denied. Instead, the reports dwell on what was legally a non-issue, the ownership of the copyrights. It is not unusual for recording contracts to stipulate that copyrights in sound recordings are owned by record companies, particularly where record companies fund the production of these recordings. Though this sort of stipulation is typical of most exclusive recording contracts, this does not by any means have to be the case. With appropriate representation artists can negotiate for reduced copyright interests on the side of the labels with whom they sign.

From my point of view, the more important questions from this case are:-

1. Why was payment of royalties to Fifty-Six Hope Road Music Limited intentionally denied?
2. What was the judge's decision on their entitlement to royalties?
3. Was there an appropriate agreement between the beneficiaries of the estate and Fifty-Six Hope Road Music Limited assigning the rights to royalties?

Unfortunately I have not had the benefit of reading the full text of the judgment. Maybe the questions I ask will be answered then, who knows.

Summary

- A greater level of awareness regarding the importance of intellectual property law and entertainment contracts needs to be encouraged.
- A reduction of the cultural resistance to operating within accepted business norms is required.

Billy Mystic lead singer, guitarist and songwriter for the band Mystic Revealers, has been a mentor for several emerging artists identified with the "Reggae Revival" © 2015 Sista Irie Photography

The Billy Mystic owned **Jamnesia** surf club became the live performance space that provided much needed opportunities for practice and exposure for young artists such as Chronixx, Protoje, Jah9, NoMaddz, Kelissa, and Kabaka Pyramid. © 2015 Sista Irie Photography

Shaggy is a perfect example of the professionalism, humility, consistency, and music business understanding that is required for international success at the highest possible level. © 2014 Sista Irie Photography

Jacob Hemphill, lead singer and guitarist of **SOJA**, one of the most successful home-grown American Reggae bands. They have collaborated with Jamaican acts such as Damian Marley. © 2014 Sista Irie Photography

Stephen Newland, lead singer and guitarist of **Rootz Underground**, one of the top touring bands from Jamaica. © 2014 Sista Irie Photography

Members of Reggae band **Pentateuch** seen here at the Sierra Nevada World Music Festival 2015 in California along with El Puru at left. El Puru is a visual artist and photographer who has been documenting the evolution of the movement in Jamaica called the Reggae Revival. © 2014 Sista Irie Photography

Members of the band **NoMaddz** at press conference during the Sierra Nevada World Music Festival 2015. NoMaddz singer Sheldon Shepherd is also lead actor in the Jamaican movie "Better Mus Come" © 2014 Sista Irie Photography

Master Reggae drummer Sly Dunbar of **Sly & Robbie**, the producers of the debut album for NoMaddz. Sly Dunbar is also responsible for introducing REGGAE ROADBLOCKS author Lloyd Stanbury to the Jamaican music industry in the early 1980s. © 2014 Sista Irie Photography

11
Entrepreneurship and Management Deficiencies in Reggae

The vast majority of participants in the Jamaican music industry operate micro businesses that are more often than not sole proprietorships or informal partnerships between two or more individuals. There is very little specialization, as most Reggae business operators carry out activities that cut across several distinct music industry functions. For example, it is not uncommon to find an artist who tries to act as his/her own songwriter, music producer, manager, publicist, music distributor and even show promoter. Recent technological developments have encouraged a new do-it-yourself approach to the business of music, with more artists avoiding traditional recording deals with third party companies. This new trend finds many artists now assuming roles formerly performed by music distributors and record labels. The need for effective enterprise development strategies and professional music business management is still very critical.

Defining Industry Roles and Occupations

Outlined here are some key music industry definitions and descriptions of functionaries that will be helpful, as we discuss management and entrepreneurial deficiencies in the Jamaican music industry.

Audio Engineers – Also called audio technicians, they include studio recording engineers, mixing engineers, and sound reinforcement engineers for live music presentations. Audio engineers deal with the use of equipment, musical instruments, computer hardware and software for the recording, mixing and reproduction of sound. Audio engineering concerns the creative and practical aspects of sounds and music. They are also responsible for the technical aspects of the recording process, such as sound quality, effects, and the mixing of the various sound components for either the production of a master recording or for presentation to live audiences.

Booking Agent – Responsible for seeking, negotiating and contracting for engagements requiring the services of performers.

Collection Societies – Collection societies or collective management organizations (CMOs) are non-profit members associations typically incorporated by virtue of company law. In the music industry, they represent the copyright and related rights interests of songwriters, music publishers, sound recording producers, and performers, by issuing licenses for public use of the works of their members, collecting licensing fees for use, and making royalty distributions to members.

Distributor (of sound recordings) – Provides warehousing, aggregation, delivery, and promotional services for sale of finished recorded entertainment products such as vinyl records, cassettes, CDs, and digital audio files.

Entertainment Attorney – Provides advice and negotiation services on matters related to intellectual property rights, and a wide range of contracts required in the production, promotion and distribution of entertainment products and services.

Executive Producer (music) – The person or entity responsible for funding the expenditures required to complete the sound recording production and packaging process. The Executive Producer owns the sound recording master produced.

Music Publishers – Represent songwriters by virtue of written agreements that authorize the publisher to administer the copyright interests of the songwriter in relation to the commercial exploitation and use of musical compositions. Good music publishers also seek to secure additional income for songs by having them covered, or used in films, games, or advertising.

Producer (Music) – The person responsible for the coordination and management of all creative inputs by vocalists, musicians and audio engineers that work on a sound recording production. Some music producers also assume responsibility for financing the sound recording production exercise, while others are engaged as independent music producers to deal solely with the coordination of the creative aspects of the studio recording process. A music producer is often a musician or audio engineer.

Producer (Live Show) – The person responsible for coordinating the creative, technical, contractual and promotional aspects of live music performance events.

Artist Personal and Business Manager – Otherwise called Artist Manager, provides career, personal, and business guidance and counseling to artists, and act as liaison and team leader of all other agents and personnel engaged to represent the artist.

Publicists – Develops and disseminates public relations and advertising materials to all media on behalf of artists and other practitioners in the entertainment industry. They are typically responsible for development and distribution of Media Kits (Electronic Press Kits/EPKs), and other activities such as the coordination of interviews, and social media management. Act as the interface and link between artists and the media.

Recording Artist – Includes vocalists (singers and deejays/rappers), as well as musicians who perform in recording studios for purposes of having their performance recorded, mixed and mastered for distribution to the public

Set Designers – Design and construct props, backdrops and other stage decoration and enhancements

Show Promoters – These are the owners, financiers and sometimes organizers of entertainment events, with the ultimate responsibility for the presentation of the event, and the engagement of all necessary service providers.

Song Writers – Include authors of lyrics (words) and composers of music (beats). Songwriters are the first owners of the copyrights in original musical compositions.

Stage Managers – Persons responsible for coordination of all activities on stage, including set changes, supervision of stage personnel, and the flow of the programme from a technical and performance standpoint.

Tour Managers – Provide coordination services with respect to planning and execution of shows on the road, including activities such as transportation, accommodation, meals, supervision of support personnel and interaction between performers, promoters and media.

Entrepreneurship and Enterprise Development

The advent of new music production, promotion and distribution technologies has created increased opportunities for music entrepreneurs to produce and deliver music products and services globally. New technologies have also presented challenges, attributed mainly to easier public access to content and the ability to share this content freely. The opportunities, challenges and hurdles presented by new technologies also provide the ideal environment for innovative music entrepreneurs to be creative and experiment with their ventures. The music industry has the feature of being one of few in which someone with little capital or connections can rise from a small home operation, to having a large-scale global impact on the culture of many people.

With today's technologies, artists, managers, music publishers, booking agents, and publicists are able to almost effortlessly enter the business of music. With a computer and web presence one is almost instantly in business. The ease with which one can enter the business of music also means that success is now much more difficult to achieve because of increased competition. In order to gain a competitive edge in the business of music, it is therefore critical that one finds the appropriate mix of passion for music with solid entrepreneurial and business principles. Those who embark on music business activities should therefore endeavor to obtain an understanding of the elements of a business plan, business structures, finance, accounting, taxation, marketing, personnel management, organizational behavior and leadership.

Whether one is a performer, songwriter, production company, artist manager, booking agent, merchandiser, record label, show promoter, publicist, radio, TV or Internet music broadcaster, one needs to be equipped with the essential tools and knowledge specific to the music industry in order to create successful ventures. The economic foundation of music business is built on principles of copyright law and the law of contacts. It is absolutely necessary therefore for business operators to employ appropriate business practices to address these critical issues. The business of music also relies for its success on effective use of the media. Appropriate and mutually beneficial relationships with the media, both traditional and new media such as the Internet, are therefore critical inputs for a successful business.

The Jamaican music scene has developed in an environment of

much informality, with insufficient emphasis placed on the application of business principles by a significant number of the individuals and firms involved. There is a scarcity of music business management training opportunities in Jamaica, and strong negative attitudes prevail among many in the Rastafari community regarding traditional capitalist business principles. Together these have been major deterrents to enterprise development in Reggae. A combination of relevant music business management training and attitudinal adjustments is required to facilitate the development of enterprise.

Management and Marketing of Creative Output

According to various studies conducted in recent decades, the Jamaican music industry is characterized by weaknesses in management and marketing. As far as music management is concerned, deficiencies are found mainly in the areas of talent management, the management of entities involved in production and delivery of music goods and services, and the management of music organizations such as copyright collection societies, musicians unions, and music trade associations.

There are thousands of individuals operating in Jamaica as recording artists, (vocalists and musicians), songwriters, and music producers. The Jamaica Federation of Musicians (musicians union), Jamaica Association of Composers Authors and Publishers, and Jamaica Music Society, together represent artists, songwriters and music producers in excess of 5,000. Many songwriters, recording artists and music producers are also not registered members of any of the above mentioned organizations. The majority of the recording artists, songwriters and music producers in Jamaica are either not managed, or are engaged in management relationships with inexperienced and unqualified talent managers.

Many sole proprietors, partnerships and small registered companies operate in Jamaica as record labels, music studios, show promoters, booking agents, publicists, merchandisers, and other traders in music goods and services. Accurate estimates of the numbers of music businesses operators are very difficult to come by, due to the informality of the Jamaican music sector. As mentioned in a previous chapter, an initiative to establish a registry for the entertainment sector was launched in 2014 by the Ministry of Tourism and Entertainment.

A number of music industry organizations have been formed in

Jamaica in recent years. These include the Jamaica Association of Composers Authors and Publisher, the Jamaica Music Society, the Recording Industry Association of Jamaica, the Jamaica Reggae Industry Association, the Jamaica Association of Vintage Artists and Affiliates, the Jamaica Reggae Industry Association, and the Jamaica Sound Systems Association. Prior to the formation of these organizations, only the Jamaica Federation of Musicians and the Performing Rights Society existed as music associations. As is the case with talent management and the management of small music enterprises, there are very significant management deficiencies within existing music organizations.

Effective music business management requires the acquisition and use of skills, concepts, and methodologies to professionally handle legal, financial, artistic, technical, and ethical issues that face contemporary music business professionals. Jamaica's music has evolved and expanded at a phenomenal rate since the 1960s, particularly from a creative point of view. Unfortunately there has not been a commensurate level of attention placed on ensuring that the required business management skills are secured and utilized. Lack of adequate management is arguably the largest single roadblock to the further development of the Jamaican music industry.

Technological innovations and new trends in entertainment consumption have resulted in business model adjustments never before witnessed in the global music industry. These changes have opened doors for small music business operators, but also bring with them new challenges. The days of reliance on the large record label as the only option of getting fans to hear your music, are gone, with the focus now shifted to the creation of, and association with, brands.[101] The Internet, social media and mobile communication explosion now provide new marketing opportunities for musicians.

The emergence in Jamaica of the movement referred to as the "Reggae Revival" is a good example of the impact of technological changes on music marketing. Relatively new Jamaican Roots Reggae artists such as Chronixx and Protoje have been able to significantly expand their global fan base and attract the attention of mainstream international media without being affiliated with third party record labels. The following

---

101. https://www.nextbigsound.com/industryreport/2014

reports on Chronixx are good examples: From the BBC[102], from NBC[103], from Billboard Magazine[104], and from NPR.[105] Protoje has also received his fair share of intentional mainstream music media recognition with articles in Billboard Magazine.[106]

In addition to Chronixx and Protoje, several other new Jamaican artists have been able to capitalize on marketing opportunities provided by the Internet, social media and mobile communication devices to reach and expand their global fan bases, to connect with traditional and online media, and to facilitate traditional and online retail sales and distribution of recordings as well as touring. Artists such as Raging Fyah, Jah9, Kabaka Pyramid, Dre Island, Jesse Royal, Iba Mahr and Kelissa, who all gained international recognition in a relatively short period of time, are good examples, as are Raging Fyah[107] and Kabaka Pyramid.[108]

Although some Reggae artists have taken advantage of opportunities presented by the Internet and new media technologies, there are still significant marketing weaknesses existing in the Jamaican music industry. Most small music business operators are not aware of, or do not utilize, the methodologies required to reach their core fans, and to communicate with them effectively. The Jamaican Reggae Revival movement has generated renewed interest in traditional roots Reggae music. In order to maximize the benefits from the digital and Internet explosion, the artists associated with this "Revival" will need the following:

1. an understanding of the foundational best practices required for successful music marketing campaigns;
2. an appreciation of the shifts and new trends in music and entertainment consumption, including changes affecting access to physical products, digital audio file downloads, and digital audio streaming;
3. an integrated approach to music marketing with focus on media (online and traditional), distribution (online and traditional), advertising, merchandising, touring, and branding.

---

102. http://www.bbc.co.uk/programmes/p01r0y8b
103. http://www.nbc.com/the-tonight-show/filters/guests/844
104. http://www.billboard.com/biz/articles/news/global/5733093/is-chronixx-jamaican-Reggaes-next-big-thing-chris-blackwell-diplo
105. http://www.npr.org/2013/12/29/256116848/jamaica-s-hottest-new-school-Reggae-artists-return-to-roots
106. http://www.billboard.com/articles/business/6538608/protoje-ancient-future-album-jamaica
107. https://www.facebook.com/raging.fyah
108. https://www.facebook.com/KabakaPyramid

4. an understanding of how online music distribution and retail works: the relevant terms, deals, formats, options, and key companies to work with;

5. knowledge of public relations services and outlets that matter— including national, regional, local, and specialized music trade publications— how and when to communicate to them, and when to hire publicity help;

6. an understanding of how radio (traditional and online) promotion works, and when it is appropriate to engage independent promotion services;

7. knowledge of what to make for merchandise, when to make it, and how much to spend.

8. a timeline and working marketing plan designed to fit the individual strengths of one's product or service.

New digital, Internet and mobile communications technologies will reduce barriers to the global distribution and promotion of Jamaican Reggae, provided that a conducive marketing environment is created and maintained to support business operators. Jamaican music business must be driven and facilitated by strategies that include the establishment of local music business institutional infrastructure to enable improvements in business awareness, and entrepreneurship, the provision of affordable access to reliable and fast Internet, real-time online transaction settlement facilities, access to capital, and greater access to mainstream international media exposure and influence over the production of relevant media content. The establishment of music business incubator facilities for small operators would be very helpful.

Training, Professional Development and Mentorship

The global music market is experiencing rapid adjustments as a result of the digital and Internet revolution. The implications are major and far reaching for music industry practitioners and the consuming public. The music industry is at the cutting edge of technical change in the emerging digital economy. Developing countries like Jamaica have a significant opportunity to be at the forefront of the digital revolution with the application of appropriate management and marketing strategies.

Unfortunately the areas of music business management and marketing have been two of the weakest aspects of the Jamaican music industry.

The further development of the Jamaican music industry will require a paradigm shift in approach to training and skills upgrading for participants in the industry. Such an approach should include the following:

1. the creation of new training opportunities to help raise skills levels across all sectors of the industry, with particular emphasis on music business management and marketing;
2. the promotion of innovative and flexible training and skills;
3. the building of the industry's commitment to life-long learning, by developing and fostering a training culture among practitioners;
4. ensuring that the education sector anticipates and responds to industry, technological and global change (The publication of research papers and other information about the industry will be crucial in accomplishing this.);
5. promotion of creativity, innovation, and capacity building, to enhance and maintain Jamaica's international cultural competitiveness.

There have been some successful mentorship initiatives implemented by experienced artists and music producers in Jamaica since the turn of the century. These include Billy Mystic's Jamnesia live music project, and Mikie Bennett's Grafton Recording Studios. Several artists and songwriters have been provided the opportunity to learn, practice and be guided through live showcase exposure, and discussion sessions hosted at Jamnesia and Grafton Studios. More opportunities like these are needed across the island.

Government Training Institutions

The Jamaican music industry is new to notions of formal training. With the exception of the Edna Manley College for the Visual and Performing Arts, most existing tertiary training programs are relatively new, and underdeveloped. The Edna Manley College emphasizes training in the creative and performance aspects of the arts, with very little focus on arts management. Under the directorship of Roger Williams, the Edna Manley College Music Department has done an excellent job in training young musicians for transition to gainful employment on the local and international live music circuit. Mr. Williams however acknowledges that the College's music business and arts management courses are inadequate.

Apart from the courses offered at Edna Manley College, there are a few other arts and entertainment management training programmes available in Jamaica at institutions such as the University of the West Indies, the University of Technology and the HEART Trust. These programmes are also weak in music business management. The economic benefits of activities in the music industry cannot be realized without adequate representation and intellectual property rights management at all levels. Priority attention should therefore be given by local training institutions to new and upgraded programs in areas such as entertainment contracts, copyright administration, music publishing, event management, artist management, and entertainment marketing.

In addition to formal training programs in music business management and marketing, there is the need for creative and innovative alternative training models to address the peculiarities of the Jamaican environment. In Jamaica most employment in the music industry is seasonal and part-time, and the vast majority of operators are small sole proprietors and informal partnerships. There also seems to be a reluctance and resistance to formal training among many persons in the Jamaican music industry. Persons tend to be more receptive to apprenticeships and mentoring.

More flexibility in the delivery of training to music business practitioners and music organizations is therefore necessary. Short courses, workshops, continuing professional development programmes, and courses tailored to specific organizational contexts are required. Training models must also of necessity seek to employ, as much as possible, the new tools that are available through the Internet, social media, and mobile communication. Special effort should be made to enlighten practitioners about the global benefits from the application of new digital and Internet technology in the business of music management and marketing.

The Jamaica Cultural Development Commission (JCDC), is a government statutory agency established and operating since 1968. Its primary responsibility is the coordination, planning and presentation of a range of national and regional arts and culture activities annually, which culminate in the grand Jamaica Independence and Festival competitions each year. Participation in JCDC activities is widespread throughout Jamaica, and includes individuals of all ages, as well as community organizations and schools. The JCDC's annual Festival song contest has been responsible for the promotion of several top Jamaican recording artists, including Toots and the Maytals, Eric Donaldson, and Desmond Dekker. The JCDC controls and manages several performance venues across the island, and as a part of its activities conducts workshops focused on the creative elements of performance and production.

In its almost 50 years of operation, the JCDC has failed to adequately address the business management, marketing and other commercial aspects of its arts and culture activities and the practitioners with whom it interacts. Several announcements have been made about the need for an adjustment to the JCDC's business model to accommodate more aspects of management and marketing. This includes an announcement by the Minister of Culture in 2014 regarding the government's decision to create a culture management division within the JCDC to provide those services. However, the view held by some Jamaican cultural industries experts is that the JCDC should instead focus on using its facilities and relationships to deliver arts and music management and marketing training in partnership with educational institutions such and the Edna Manley College of the Visual and Performing Arts, and the University of the West Indies.

Entertainment management training is financially prohibitive for most Jamaican practitioners, many of whom are self-employed. The provision of staff training support is also difficult for small organizations that are usually cash strapped. Many arts organizations around the world have benefited from capacity building support from government, as well as local and international donors. These realities underpin the need for creative funding programs for training in the music and entertainment industries in Jamaica.

Despite studies having identified management and marketing as major weaknesses in the Jamaican entertainment industry, and frequent calls by local practitioners for the implementation of measures to provide relevant training, enough has not been done to effect change. Political and business leaders inside Jamaica have continued to render lip-service about the value and importance of the music industry to the social and economic development of Jamaica. There is no evidence of a commitment to address the weaknesses in management and marketing capacity.

Linkages with Other Sectors – Film, Visual Arts, Dance, Fashion, Food

The challenges faced by the global recording industry because of technological changes have resulted in increased emphasis on alternative business models and income streams for musicians and music distributors. The alignment of music with films, video games, visual arts, fashion, and food, has taken on new significance. The importance of the film and video sector to Jamaica's music industry is underscored by the success of the first major feature film The Harder They Come produced in 1972 and starring international Reggae star Jimmy Cliff. The launch of The Harder They Come is regarded by many as the catalyst that propelled Jamaican popular music into the international arena.

Since The Harder They Come a very vibrant film and video production sector aligned to music has emerged in Jamaica. A significant number of promotional music videos of relatively high quality are produced annually in Jamaica and used primarily as tools to generate awareness and demand for artists and their music. Other aspects of the visual arts, such as still photography, art and design, have also been closely integrated with music production and marketing. The integration of visual arts in the form of designs for music releases, events, band logos, and merchandise, played a significant role in the appeal of the young roots artists associated with the Reggae Revival movement.

As is the case with music, the visual arts sector is also hampered by ignorance and confusion regarding the management of the rights associated with the production and dissemination of visual and audio-visual works. Issues related to copyrights and trademarks continue to be mismanaged. The lines of demarcation regarding the rights of photographers and the right to privacy of individuals remain blurred and therefore result in many disputes.

Jamaican popular music has influenced and been closely associated with local dance, fashion and food. Rastafarian dietary practices, such as eating vegetarian, and preparing meals without salt and other chemicals, commonly referred to as "ital food", are closely aligned to Reggae music. The concept of Jamaican "Jerk" has now been incorporated in festival celebrations in Jamaica as well as in several immigrant Caribbean communities in North America. The leading Reggae music distributor in the world – VP Music Group – is sponsor/partner of "Jerk" music festivals in the USA. So is the largest food distribution company in Jamaica, Grace Kennedy.[109]

Jamaican dance and fashion associated with Reggae have been exposed to international audiences over the past several decades through various means. It is not uncommon to find Jamaican dance moves and fashion trends incorporated in the works of fashion houses and music/dance performers internationally. Management of these linkages for the benefit of local creators and presenters has been weak and ad hoc in most instances. As in the case of other creative activity in Jamaica, there is a tendency to celebrate and boast about dance and fashion trends of local origin, with not enough emphasis on managing rights for the benefit of the people who create.

Tourism and Music

The management of the Jamaican tourism sector and its relationship with music has been the source of much debate and contention for many years. The tourism sector has been the largest earner of foreign currency for the Jamaican economy. Economic studies indicate that the contribution of music and entertainment to the value of the Jamaican tourism product rates higher than other non-music sectors that receive significant funding and other development support. There are strong arguments in favour of a close link and collaboration between the tourism and music and entertainment sectors, but on the other hand significant reservations have also been expressed. There is the view that priority should be given to the promotion and support of local culture to build more domestic awareness and appreciation, and to provide benefits and enjoyment for the local population.

The dilemma of the tourism and music/entertainment collaborative pursuit is exemplified in the often competitive relationship between the Ministry of Tourism and Entertainment, Ministry of Culture, and Ministry of Industry and Commerce. The availability of significant amounts of promotional dollars within the Tourism Ministry, and the manner in which these funds are used, has come into question from time to time by

---

109. https://www.facebook.com/JamaicanJerkFestivalFLA

members of the local music and entertainment community.[110] There have also been clear instances of conflict where members of the directorship of government tourism agencies have simultaneously served as directors and or shareholders of private companies in the concert and events promotion business that benefit from government tourism sponsorship funding. Jamaican tourism agencies have also provided large sums of money in the sponsorship of events that promote non-Jamaican music, such as the Jamaica Jazz & Blues Festival, while other events which highlight local music, get far less funding, and sometimes no funding.

There appears to be a major disconnect between the marketing initiatives of the Jamaican tourism agencies, and the promotion of Reggae in the international markets of Europe and North America. Very little collaboration exists between the local tourism agencies and the numerous international Reggae festivals in Europe and North America. There is strong argument that the contribution of Reggae to Jamaica's tourism product and to building awareness about Jamaica as a destination is grossly undervalued by the Jamaican government and private interests in tourism. In 2014, initiatives announced by the Ministry of Tourism and Entertainment to engage touring artists to help promote Jamaica met with mixed reactions. Music industry practitioners argue that touring artists are already doing a great job in promoting Jamaica internationally, and that the government's emphasis should on the provision of assistance to make local artists better able to compete with their international counterparts who now dominate the Reggae touring circuit.[111]

Summary

- There is an urgent need for clarity regarding the roles and responsibilities of various functionaries and occupations in the music industry.
- Greater focus on, and appreciation of the trends and opportunities in the music industry resulting from rapid technological changes is necessary.
- Business operations need to be formalized and structured.
- National, regional and global marketing strategies need to be devel-

---

110. http://www.jamaicaobserver.com/entertainment/Slashed_15746252
111. http://www.jamaicaobserver.com/news/Tourism-Ministry-seeks-support-of-artistes-in-promoting-island

oped and utilized by individuals, firms and music associations.

- Mentorships, incubators and music clusters need to be encouraged.
- Training institutions need to place more emphasis on incorporating active music business practitioners in training programmes.
- More business development linkages between music operators and operators in the tourism and technology sectors are required.

Removing Reggae Roadblocks

I n previous chapters I examined critical elements restricting the development of a more viable Jamaican music industry nationally and globally. This final chapter provides my perspective on the question of whether Reggae business roadblocks are self-imposed by artists and supporting service providers or created externally.

As I have argued, Reggae music is primarily born and nurtured through the struggles of a displaced people fighting to survive within an environment that is subject to prejudice, discrimination, and cultural conflicts. A very significant amount of the issues addressed in the lyrical content of Reggae music speaks to injustice, discrimination, and the desire of former African slaves to connect with their roots, and experience a united Africa. Bob Marley became the iconic representation of these messages. In any discussion of the development of the Reggae music industry, the impact of Rastafari and the use of marijuana cannot be ignored. Reports of the inhumane treatment and persecution of members of the Rastafari and Reggae music communities by agents of the Jamaican government are well documented. Prominent examples include accounts of incidents such as the Pinnacle raids in the 1940s and 1950s, the Coral Gardens massacre in 1963, and police brutality and abuse inflicted on numerous Reggae artists, most notably Peter Tosh for his outspoken and militant stance against government corruption and manipulation.[112]

---

112. http://www.independent.co.uk/arts-entertainment/music/features/move-over-bob-marley-peter-tosh-is-finally-getting-the-recognition-he-deserves-8914028.htm

The ongoing conflict between agents of the state, such as the police, and the perception of some government representatives that Reggae artists are disorganized disruptive elements, have caused a major barrier of mistrust between artists and state officials. A common sentiment expressed by Rastafarian artists is that the Jamaican government is a puppet of the Queen of England and American political leaders, and willingly bows to multinational corporations that seek to exploit Jamaica's human talents and natural resources. The Rastafari and Reggae community is also very critical of the IMF and its impact on Jamaica. The consistent promotion of these sentiments in music and everyday speech by many Reggae artists has widened the mistrust gap, further obstructing cooperation and collaboration between government and the artists. Many Jamaican artists regard government as the local representative of the Babylon system that fights against Rastafari and other free-thinking descendants of Africa, thus making government/artist cooperation and partnerships problematic. Popular songs such as Well Done by Reggae Revivalist Kabaka Pyramid provide a good example.[113]

In an effort to gain the support of the Rastafari community, the Jamaican government has made provisions within the law to decriminalize marijuana, whereby sacramental use by Rasta has been sanctioned. This legal provision is however not without controversy. The Jamaican government through its Tourism Enhancement Fund, has also supported the mounting of a major Rastafari exhibition on the island. This initiative received the endorsement of several members of the Rastafari community, as a step in the right direction.[114]

Over the years, successive Jamaican government administrations have highlighted the informality and fragmented nature of the local music industry as a major deterrent to public/private development cooperation and investments. While recognizing this as a legitimate barrier, it is my view that not enough has been done by government to encourage and facilitate capacity building and increased awareness among industry practitioners, in order to reduce informality and fragmentation. Informality and industry fragmentation remain the reality, despite the findings of studies that identify the lack of business knowledge and the

---

113. https://www.youtube.com/watch?v=kLteujzg6Mc

114. http://www.jamaicaobserver.com/news/TEF-funds-historic-Rastafari-exhibition-at-Museum-West_18899069

inadequate governance capacity of music organizations as major barriers to development. There is clearly need for more emphasis to be placed on music business education and arts management in the government's education policy. There appears to be a very narrow perspective of what constitutes music business management, and although there has been much talk, not enough action has been taken by government supported educational institutions.[115]

The impasse between some members of the music industry and the government of Jamaica has no doubt played a very significant role in stifling the domestic and international growth and sustainability of Jamaican Reggae business operators. The lack of a comprehensive national music industry development policy facilitates the continued existence of a number of barriers to development, but government insensitivity and/or inactivity is not the only barrier.

The development and global exposure of Reggae is a process with complex historical, socio-political, cultural, and business related issues. These issues are often manifested in the form of self-imposed roadblocks to adequate development of Jamaica's music industry.

Rastafari Versus Babylon

While the Rastafari movement can legitimately claim to be one of, if not the most significant contributor to the development and advancement of Reggae globally, there are certain aspects of Rastafari lifestyle and philosophy that have worked against business development in Reggae. The refusal or reluctance of many Reggae artists and music producers to negotiate and sign contracts with regard to their business and creative relationships has been a major contributor to misunderstandings, conflicts, and unfair commercial exploitation of their musical works. The Rastafari philosophy that projects the belief that contracts and business deals are tools of the Babylon system, and should be avoided, creates a significant barrier to business development.

The principle that Reggae music is strictly about doing Jah's work, and that Rasta is not interested in Babylon commercialization, is also contradictory. While many Rastafarian artists often subscribe to this view, they also engage in informal business negotiations and deals where they insist on being paid large sums of money in exchange for their recording

---

115. http://jamaica-gleaner.com/gleaner/20140218/ent/ent2.html

and/or live performance services. They don't work for free. In fact, some of the most militant and outspoken Rasta Reggae artists charge the highest fees for their recording services and live shows.

According to the 2014 report of the International Federation of the Phonographic Industry (IFPI), the top ten popular music markets in the world were:

1. United States of America
2. Japan
3. United Kingdom
4. Germany
5. France
6. Australia
7. Canada
8. Brazil
9. Italy
10. Holland

With the exception of the live Reggae music scene in some African countries, the above mentioned top ten markets also provide the most lucrative business opportunities for touring and sales of recorded Reggae music. There is evidence of resistance to certain Rastafari messages[116] in Reggae music from some of these countries. In particular there appears to be resistance by some to messages that speak to the divinity of His Imperial Majesty Emperor Haile Selassie, homosexuality, and the colonial and post-colonial oppressive and manipulative tactics of representatives of the Babylon system.

The Jamaican Rastafari community has suffered over the years from a high level of disunity among its various mansions, as well as open disputes and confrontations between leading Rastafari individuals. Individuality and differences in philosophy have been common features of Rastafari. Many Reggae artists who identify with Rastafari have carried these traits into their music activities, resulting in their re-

---

116. Linda Aïnouche suggests that while the music is widely accepted, there are barriers to Reggae, and hints that these may be related to its role in the development of social consciousness and building bridges between black people. Aïnouche, Linda. Reggae, A Force for Dialogue. "UN Chronicle", The Magazine of the United Nations, Vol. XLIX No. 3, September 2012. http://unchronicle.un.org/article/Reggae-force-dialogue/

sistance to formalized group representation. In recent years there has been some evidence of a shift away from this individualistic approach, by the group of young Rastafarian artists identified as the Reggae Revivalists, who often project an image of unity as a collective of artists. However, many Reggae Revivalists remain handicapped by their inability to recognize the differences between Rastafari and the business of Reggae, and have therefore been unable to function in both worlds effectively and without conflicts.

Roadblocks from Cultural Diversity and Cultural Conflicts

The protection and promotion of the diversity of cultural expressions forms the basis of the UNESCO Convention of 2005. This Convention has so far been signed by over 130 countries, including Jamaica, with notable absentees being the United States and Israel.

The Rastafari belief system has had a significant impact on Jamaica since the early 1930s. Afrocentric cultural, spiritual, and socio-political perspectives emanating from Rasta philosophy have become a part of Jamaican cultural expressions. Music by Jamaican artists that include these expressions have experienced resistance in some parts of North America and Western Europe.

There are those within the North American music market who have expressed the view that the militant and spiritual messages of Rastafari in Reggae have been barriers to mainstream acceptance of Reggae music in the USA. In justification of their view, they point to the growth in popularity of home-grown American Reggae bands, such as SOJA and Rebelution, who record and perform softer less Afrocentric lyrics that appeal to a wider demographic.

The Jamaican society is built on a foundation of Christian influences and African traditions that significantly impact its culture and cultural expressions. It is an accepted part of Jamaican culture to speak out against homosexuality, and this has been reflected in the lyrical content of recordings and performances by several Reggae artists. There is a legitimate case to be made that some Jamaican recording and performing artists have included messages in their music that suggest that violent acts should be inflicted on homosexuals. The promotion of violence against gays is not the policy of the Jamaican government, and is resisted by many Jamaicans, as well as in many countries where these artists seek to present their musical works. A case can also be made that there have been attempts to suppress the protection and promotion of cultural expressions in some countries in relation to the anti-homosexuality views of Jamaican artists who do not advocate violence. The cultural conflicts presented by diverse views on homosexuality have been a major roadblock for Reggae business development in some of the top music markets of the world, particularly in North America and Western Europe.

Gangsters and Crime as Roadblocks

In recent years there have been several reports in the Jamaican and international media about prominent Jamaican Reggae artists allegedly associated with criminal activities ranging from illicit drug trafficking, to murder, firearm offenses and money laundering. The fear of widespread international crime and acts of terrorism have also resulted in significantly increased surveillance and collaboration between immigration and law enforcement authorities in North American and western European countries. As a result many Jamaican artists and music producers have been subjected to higher levels of scrutiny in their applications for entry permits to work and visit these countries. Several prominent Jamaican artists have been denied entry permits to the USA, Canada, and the UK. In these circumstances the movement of creative personnel from Jamaica into major international music markets has been severely hampered, with a crippling effect on the promotion and presentation of Jamaican Reggae in these markets.

Impact of Globalization and Technology

The increased movement of people and information facilitated by improved methods of transportation and new digital technology has created opportunities and challenges for small creative entrepreneurs in countries like Jamaica. Global travel and communication in the 20th and 21st centuries have facilitated cultural exchanges and increased the transfer of cultural practices between countries. Globalization and rapid changes in technology better enables non-Jamaicans to competitively produce and present Reggae internationally. Home grown Reggae bands from North America, the Caribbean, Europe and Latin America have demonstrated that they are capable of outselling Jamaican Reggae artists in places such as the USA, Canada, Germany, UK, France, Brazil, and Japan.

Despite advances in Internet and mobile communication technologies, access costs remain relatively high for the average user from inner city and deep rural communities in Jamaica. While many Jamaican artists and managers are online and connected with mobile communication devices, they are not as effective as they should be. In order to be globally competitive, and to grow the Reggae music industry, it is imperative that emphasis be placed on affordable access to new technologies.

Relevant training for artists and music entrepreneurs in Jamaica and other developing countries is critical for the effective use of new technologies. Digital and Internet technologies have made it potentially easier for musicians and small entrepreneurs in countries like Jamaica to produce, promote and present their products and services beyond geographic boundaries.

Failure to address the technological needs of music business operators in developing countries like Jamaica will prove to be the single largest barrier to the growth of business. If we fail to embrace and effectively use new technology, the benefits to be derived from the creative economies of developing countries like Jamaica will remain nothing but a dream.

National and International Institutional Framework

Weak management and governance capacity of music associations, and ineffective rights enforcement systems, have been identified by several studies as barriers to industry development.

In 1993 Jamaica enacted a new copyright law which facilitated the further development of music rights administration and enforcement. The new law resulted in the establishment of the Jamaica Intellectual Property Office, (JIPO), a government agency functioning as a central focal point for the administration of Intellectual Property (IP) in Jamaica. The 1993 copyright law also enabled the establishment of the Jamaica Association of Composers, Authors and Publishers, (JACAP), a national collective management organization for songwriters, and music publishers, and the formation of a collective management organization for music producers in the Jamaica Music Society, (JAMMS).

JIPO has done a good job in producing relevant educational materials and the facilitation of information dissemination with a view to sensitizing the owners of rights, users of music, and the general public. Despite JIPO's efforts there is still a significant level of ignorance and low appreciation for the value of music and the rights of composers, producers, and performers in Jamaica. Music piracy continues openly on the streets of Jamaica, and the enforcement of rights through the courts rarely pursued.

With the exception of the establishment of copyright and related rights music collection societies, members of the Jamaican music industry have failed miserably in their efforts to establish and maintain effective and properly administered music trade associations. Ignorance, mistrust, rumor mongering, and inadequate administrative skills have been major barriers to the sustainability of initiatives to establish and maintain trade associations.

In recent years the effectiveness and continued existence of music organizations such as the Recording Industry Association of Jamaica/RIAJam and the Jamaica Reggae Industry Association/JaRIA have been severely compromised by internal and external political manipulation.[117] This has resulted in the suspension of what was intended to be the annual Reggae Academy Awards, persistent struggles to establish an effective umbrella organization with a wide spectrum of industry support, and conflicts regarding the scope, purpose, and management of Jamaica's annual Reggae Month series of activities.[118]

There have been long delays restricting efforts to secure amendments and upgrades to the Jamaican copyright law to deal with new digital and Internet technologies, and to expand protection by collective management organizations to include performing artists. At the end of 2014 there was still no collective management organization in Jamaica representing the interests and rights of music performers. The impact of existing music rights collective management organizations such as JACAP and JAMMS is less than desirable. Many music producers, songwriters and music publishers in Jamaica are reluctant to become members. Reluctance seems to stem from a combination of ignorance about the role played by these organizations, and reports and rumors of internal management deficiencies.

---

117. https://www.facebook.com/notes/lloyd-stanbury/jamaica-music-cluster-jaria-and-singapore/455021115354

118. https://www.facebook.com/notes/lloyd-stanbury/Reggae-month-and-black-history-month/10155645445415355

Jamaica's inadequate internal institutional framework has negative external implications, as international cooperation with counterpart rights management and regulatory organizations and compatibility with the international music rights management systems are compromised. Jamaican music rights holders continue to complain about ineffective monitoring and collections from use of Jamaican music content by international broadcasters.

International trademark protection for Jamaican brands is still challenging, due to the fact that Jamaica is yet to subscribe to the international treaties for protection of trademarks. There needs to be more informed interventions by the Jamaican Ministry of Foreign Affairs and Trade in their deliberations in bilateral and multilateral agreements that impact trade in cultural goods and services.

Business Informality as a Roadblock

The educational system in Jamaica and most developing countries is not structured to facilitate business development within the the arts and culture sectors. While there is music and other creative activities incorporated in the formal school programs, in many instances the arts are treated as extra-curricular activities in schools, and not given the same level of attention as traditional courses such as mathematics, science, history, languages, and sports. There is also very little emphasis placed in secondary and tertiary institutions on the business and management aspects of the arts.

The arts and arts education continue to be stigmatized in the Jamaican education system, despite the fact that Reggae artists have proven that music provides viable careers and business options for various types of creative, technical and management personnel. Deficiencies in the formal educational system have contributed significantly to the unacceptable levels of informality in the local music industry.

A large percentage of Reggae practitioners are ignorant of the business principles relevant to the music and entertainment industries. Music production, promotion, distribution and presentation activities are often conducted with little or no regard for issues such as the negotiation and signing of contracts. Many artists engage unqualified and inexperienced friends and family to work with them, which usually results in a very high level of unprofessionalism.

There is also the tendency of Jamaican Reggae artists to encourage hangers-on within their work space. Lack of respect for time and punctuality are some of the outcomes of the very informal approach taken by many Jamaican Reggae artists and business operators. Failure to develop and maintain professional relationships with entertainment journalists and media personnel, and the poor attitudes of artists and management in their interpersonal communications are also business development roadblocks resulting from informality.

There is less than adequate appreciation for the principles of intellectual property rights, and in particular copyrights, among Jamaican Reggae business operators. Most Reggae artists, producers, show promoters, and managers are ignorant about basic copyright principles, and often confuse the various rights involved in the business of music, and the support organizations they need to be affiliated with. There is also very little appreciation for the value of expert knowledge and representation, which is often regarded as unwanted interference, or an unnecessary additional expense.

Roadblocks in Entrepreneurship and Business Development

The informality of the Jamaican Reggae music industry and the lack of understanding of music business principles have served as deterrents to investment in music and entertainment business ventures. At the domestic level entrepreneurs have been reluctant to participate in major business development initiatives because of the informal nature of the sector, as well as their lack of understanding of the complexities involved. At the international level entrepreneurs are reluctant to partner with unprofessional Jamaican Reggae artists, music producers, and managers.

The inadequacies of the formal education system in Jamaica regarding training in entrepreneurship and arts and entertainment business management, have worked against the development of properly run small business enterprises in Reggae. Traditional education and training programs need to be modified to cater more to creating entrepreneurs, instead of training persons to be good employees. Not enough emphasis is placed in Jamaica on extending business development facilities, including funding, to include music and entertainment operators. The economic value of copyrights is not fully appreciated or respected by the Jamaican banking system.

More private ventures that provide mentorship and business development opportunities are needed. The Nanook project in Kingston is a great example of the kind of clustering and business incubator support that is necessary on an island wide scale.[119]

The Role of Government

Several international organizations have highlighted the potential of developing countries with competitive cultural assets to benefit from economic growth and employment generation through strategic development of their creative industries. In 2010 the United Nations Conference on Trade and Development (UNCTAD) published its Creative Economy Report.[120] In 2013 the United Nations Educational Scientific and Cultural Organization (UNESCO) and the United Nations Development Programme, (UNDP) partnered in the publication of their Creative Economy Report[121]. These international initiatives emphasize the importance of the partnership and facilitatory role to be played by governments. UNESCO has played a leading role in the promotion of culture as a centerpiece of development, and calls for governments in developing countries like Jamaica to place culture high on the agenda for sustainable development. [122]

Despite Jamaica's globally recognized competitive advantage in the production and presentation of music, and in the face of recommendations made in several economic reports conducted by local and international experts, there is still no comprehensive national development policy or implementation strategy in place for the Jamaican Reggae music industry. Successive Jamaican administrations appear to be either reluctant to implement appropriate strategies, or ignorant to the real economic value of Jamaican music and culture.

The issues discussed in this chapter clearly reveal areas in which government intervention is necessary. In the face of all the evidence provided, one is forced to ponder the real reason for Jamaican government

---

119. http://www.nanookonline.com

120. http://unctad.org/en/pages/PublicationArchive.aspx?publicationid=946

121. http://www.unesco.org/new/en/culture/themes/creativity/creative-economy-report-2013-special-edition/

122. https://www.youtube.com/watch?v=mWS3UPqm9iU

resistance or failure to support the structured development of the Reggae music industry. Many argue that successive Jamaican governments have placed the interests of big local and international investors ahead of cultural development and preservation. This argument is also supported by the view that artists, particularly Reggae artists, are known to be very critical of the exploitative and discriminatory practices of colonial and post-colonial Jamaican governments and their big business partners. After many years of work focused on the growth and development of the Reggae music industry, it is my opinion that the Jamaican government's failure to adequately facilitate the development of the creative industries is the result of incompetence and corruption among state administrators and their technical advisors. There is also no evidence of the political will to place culture at the forefront of economic development in Jamaica.

The development of the Jamaican music industry has also been hampered by misunderstanding by some music industry players of the role of government. It is not uncommon to witness very strong objection from Reggae artists to the participation of government in the music industry development process. Many people in the music business mistakenly interpret government facilitation and the provision of necessary support as actual participation by government in the business of music. There is mistrust of government by artists and this is understandable as far as artistic license and censorship issues are concerned. It is however possible to open doors for opportunities to elevate the country and artists with strategically structured private/public partnerships that include increased education, international promotion and other necessary supporting infrastructure.

As is the case in many other countries, Jamaican creative practitioners and the state face the challenge of reconciling the development of the arts for purposes of presentation, awareness building and preservation, and the development of the arts as business and industry. The effectiveness of the government and private sector in music industry development in Jamaica has been hampered as a consequence of our inability to design and implement policies catering to cultural awareness, preservation and presentation, that can co-exist with and enhance business development.

Perspectives from Interviews:

Identifying and attempting to find solutions to the roadblocks to the Jamaican Reggae industry needs several perspectives. While I have quoted and cited various views and information sources, the following opinions of some knowledgeable players involved in Reggae music give strength and balance to this work.

Warren Smith – CEO of Sierra Nevada World Music Festival

The primary challenge for Reggae is to develop strong song-writing abilities that will allow the music to reach out to a larger audience. This was prevalent with Bob Marley and many of the Reggae artists that came out of the 1970s. With great songs there is no end to success.

A growing barrier to Reggae, at least in the U.S., has been the increasing regulation of foreign artists with the aid of new technologies. Work visa requirements have become much more stringent, and the cost relatively expensive for most foreign artists. Artists can no longer travel and perform in the U.S. as tourists, which is how many artists entered the U.S. in the past century. In addition to work visa requirements, there is also the responsibility of foreign musicians to deal with taxation issues. The U.S currently requires promoters to withhold 30 percent of an artists' fee for tax purposes. I do believe this will increasingly deprive many artists of the opportunity to perform in the U.S. Artists that have neglected to pay taxes over the years will soon confront obstacles to performing in the U.S.

Government in Jamaica can play a very large role, as it does in many other countries through their arts councils and cultural departments. For instance, Australia, New Zealand, Korea, China and many other countries aid their artists to spread their message world-wide. These countries often subsidize the artist's travel costs. One thing that could possibly be helpful for Jamaican artists would be the creation of a government agency to aid Jamaican artists in their attempts to perform abroad. There also needs to be more emphasis on music business education in Jamaica. Artists and management need to learn more about the visa and tax requirements in foreign countries, and how to best assist Artists with these issues. No one is doing an artist a favor to have him/ her fall into an IRS tax maze.

The continued role of Reggae music throughout the world will depend on the artists, management and government working together to meet the challenges.

Neville Garrick – Bob Marley Art Director

In this struggle of music and otherwise, education is the key to liberation.

If you are not educated you will depend on someone else to guide you in certain things that you don't know. Apart from Lloyd Stanbury, I don't know if there are any other lawyers from Jamaica who are music business lawyers. Music business law is different from criminal law and general litigation. It is a law unto itself, and based on my experience living in Hollywood the entertainment capital of the world, people will sell you out to the highest bidder. It is therefore necessary to have a good lawyer, or good representation from someone knowledgeable that you trust.

The new crop of cultural artists coming out of Jamaica, such as Chronixx, Protoje, Kabaka Pyramid, Kelissa, and Raging Fyah, remind me of the seventies when we had people like Culture, Burning Spear, Bob Marley, Peter Tosh and Bunny Wailer. They have uplifted me so much. After Bob, it wasn't Bunny Wailer who was the next big thing. It was Yellow Man. We have been on a slippery slope ever since. So now I really see a resurgence. These new cultural artists seem to be well educated. They are not idiots who play by luck, or are just trying a thing. As I have been quoted before as saying, the future is in good hands, because there are at least seven of these youths that will carry on the struggle. They don't look like youths who will bow to Hollywood business to reach superstar status, but will stick to their craft.

With regard to Reggae and the mainstream music market, I don't think we have to "crossover". Artists like Sean Paul have teamed with black American artists such as Beyonce to make that "crossover", but in my opinion Reggae is strong enough and we don't have to water it down.

I remember when people complained about "Exodus" and said Rasta gone funky, but when it was declared album of the century, everyone jumped onboard and loved it. Bob was just way ahead of his time. What he was trying to do was to get played on R&B radio in America, as in those days there was almost none, and we still get almost none today.

213

We need to look at who is really buying Reggae. It's mostly white college kids, the same ones who bought Bob Marley and Peter Tosh records. We should try to focus promotion to those kids, to the colleges. College radio stations still exist.

The Government of Jamaica has a very large role to play which they have underplayed from the very beginning until now. For example, Reggae Sunsplash was started in 1978, and turned Jamaica into a summer vacation spot. With all the success of Bob Marley, Peter Tosh, Burning Spear etc., the government has never built a venue specifically for music in Jamaica in the range of 2,000, 3,000 or 5,000 audience capacity.

There was an initiative many years ago where the government identified lands opposite the National Stadium for the development of what was then called "Celebrity Park". I even designed something in the shape of a guitar for a performance center for that site, but nothing materialized.

The National Arena which is used for many live music events in Kingston was never built with any intention to have music in it. The National Arena was built for the 1966 Commonwealth Games to host basketball, volleyball and other indoor sports. This is one area where the government has fallen short. For all the revenue that music has brought into Jamaica via tourism, they should have invested long ago in building a proper venue. Government should also provide a supportive environment to create more musicians, by allowing free import access to musical instruments, and ensuring that every high school incorporates music as a formal part of their curriculum. This would allow for the education of youths about the creative   aspects of music as well as the business aspects of music.

It recently came to my attention that some people are of the view that there is resistance to Rastafari messages in Reggae. That is news to me, as when I look at crowds at European Reggae festivals such as Rototom, I see lots of Rasta flags in the audience. Establishment radio and media have never played Reggae. Some people said Bob "sold out" when he recorded "Turn Your Lights Down Low" and other similar songs, but this was done to get played at 4 in the afternoon.

If you are a fisherman you have to put a little bait on the hook. So we released the "Kaya" album which was a more pop kind of album, and *when we had them listening, he came with his hardest album "Survival". You cannot make the resistance stop you. Rasta never get weary yet. Resistance is nothing new.*

Today's kids have an advantage with access to the Internet, but not everyone is using it effectively. The advent of the Internet affords youths the opportunity to learn, do research and access information which I had to do in my time by visiting libraries at universities. The only thing I knew about African history as a young adult was what I was told by the Rastaman. Access to the Internet and effective use of social media also enables today's artist to take charge of the promotion and distribution of their recorded music, rather than rely entirely on record labels. Education is the key to liberation.

In my opinion the government of Jamaica does have a major role to play in the further development of the music industry, but I don't know if they really see it.

Dermot Hussey – Radio Producer & DJ at SiriusXM Radio

SOME REALITIES: The biggest seller of music, Apple's iTunes is reporting a drop of between 13 percent and 14 percent worldwide in its sales in 2014, caused, the Wall Street Journal says, by the availability of cheap music from free videos and streaming.

The rise of the American Reggae artist, at home, in the same year has a bearing on those figures, because they outsell their Jamaican counterparts, meaning that even in a depressed market, they are doing better. They also have an advantage, in the area of live shows, where traditionally most Jamaican acts make their money. The American Reggae groups have a built in advantage, a home audience that they have developed, making it possible for them to tour all year, and they don't need visas. Can Jamaican Reggae acts continue to regard Reggae as summer music, when a handful tour and the rest make festival appearances?

Insofar as the business of music is concerned, there is a need for a better understanding of the administration, as it relates to the world economy. An understanding of the changes, from vinyl to digital, back to vinyl; how that impacts the bottom line. Knowing the technology and its application to music; understanding the financial trends of music sales, performance income, global strength, awareness, branding and marketing.

In order for the Jamaican Reggae artist to assimilate into the pop world, they have to know what core values of the music they need to retain, but also expand on the intelligence of the lyrical content; melodies, and how to use the new trends, visuals and digital concepts.

There are also some great challenges that have been ongoing for a long time. The question of "rights" who owns what, as it refers to catalogues. Attitudes: hustling and corruption, which speak for themselves. The biggest challenges for the creatives, is the need for a top studio/artist development facility that can deliver a finished talent and product."

Wayne Jobson – Musician, Attorney at Law, Radio DJ

Bob Marley and Peter Tosh gave up their lives for Reggae music. It is not something to be taken lightly. They were crusaders on a mission from God. Reggae has a frequency that touches and moves people across the planet, even those who don't speak English are able to understand Marley and Tosh's brilliant lyrics.

Jamaica captured lightening in a bottle, but we have squandered it over the past 20 years with mindless, moronic songs about sex and guns. We swapped Africa Unite for Cake Soap and skin bleaching. Thankfully, a few original foundation soldiers like Steel Pulse and The Abyssinians have kept the torch burning. And a new army has arisen in Chronixx, Jah Bouks, Protoje to give us some hope for the future.

Reggae is not lacking in talent. NO ONE can sing better than Barrington Levy. It's hard to find a better performer than Luciano, or a tighter band than Third World. What is lacking in Reggae is songwriting, management, and attitude.

First, songwriting: What happened to the genius songs of the 70s and 80s? "I Need a Roof", "What is Life", "Cottage in Negril", "Tide is High"? What we need in Jamaica is a school just for songwriting, to study with the masters who wrote these great songs. Let's have Professor Bob Andy teaching the masterpiece "I've Got to go Back Home". Our music and culture have been taken to greater heights by foreigners like Rebelution from California and Soldiers of Jah Army (SOJA) from Washington DC. These bands play roots Reggae and sell out 10,000 seaters around the world because they write good songs with uplifting messages.

Secondly, management: Most Reggae artists have their brother, friend or wife managing them, who know nothing about radio, touring, press or marketing abroad. They therefore stay within the small Jamaican circuit overseas. One needs experienced managers with know-how and contacts to make one into a star. We need a music management school.

Thirdly, attitude: Because we have very few movie stars, TV stars, or sports stars (Bolt excepted) in Jamaica, all the focus is on the music stars. As soon as an artist has one minor local hit, they think that they are the new Bob Marley. They demand huge fees and have entourages of 50 people. Meanwhile worldwide they have sold 50 CDs. Someone needs to coach these musicians, like the brilliant Glen Mills does for Bolt.

Our musicians need to have a vision, a unique style, and find their own voice. They need to do storytelling with texture and fabric. This is a passion, not a hustle. We need to create teams with band members, management, producers etc., as no one can do it alone. We need to create a global family of fans who feel that camaraderie with our music and each other. Only bands that have created families have become huge and lasted. Bob Marley, Jimmy Buffett, The Grateful Dead etc.

Coxone never had any help from the government to build Studio One. Blackwell never had any help from the government to market Bob Marley. The government can help by supporting the music schools and sponsoring shows through the Tourist Board. But it is up to the musicians to uplift Reggae music, reclaim our birthright and recapture lightning in a bottle.

Elliott Leib – Music Producer, Label Executive

Bob Marley said that Reggae would continue to grow until if found its rightful and proper audience. In 2015 the Reggae beat underpins or influences huge swaths of the popular music landscape. Many of today's artists associated with Reggae's growth and varieties are one or more generations removed from the "golden age" of the 1970s. Many hail from North America and Europe and have a more ideological rather than an ethnic or religious commitment to Rastafari concepts and practices. Elsewhere, where poorer peoples have adopted Reggae to express and comment on their own anti-colonial heritage(s), the musical tradition *grows and develops with other textures, e.g. Maori Reggae from New Zealand.*

Rastafari roots Reggae will always be linked to its origins in Jamaica. Today and forever, Reggae artists from Jamaica should be proud of this indelible, homegrown contribution. They should be challenged to make music worthy of sustaining and growing this great tradition regardless of any other popular culture trends. These same artists and musicians should also recognize that the worldwide appeal of Reggae varies by territory and market. If Jamaican Reggae artists want to reach audiences internationally their musical abilities and business practices have to be of a world standard if they want a place at the table.

Jamaican popular music can trend towards the bipolar. On the one hand, when radios and jukeboxes mattered in the development of sound systems culture, every aspect of world popular culture entered into the mix. Country and Western lyrics would surface in the most recent rendition of a cover of a top 10 American soul tune, and so on. On the other hand, Jamaican music can also be insular and parochial. How many non-Jamaicans are really interested in the "Gully" versus "Gaza" type of Dancehall subculture?

Summary

- Greater and more affordable access to technology and training in appropriate use is required.
- More effective government intervention in the promotion and negotiation of agreements affecting international trade in cultural goods and services is required
- The development and presentation of appropriate courses in the management of cultural industries is a priority need.
- The role of traditional and new media in music industry development needs to be emphasized and relationships with media functionaries improved.
- The industry needs to develop means to attract investment through (a) training in entrepreneurship (b) enlightening funders on the financial value of copyrights, and (c) the implementation of tax incentives.
- There is an urgent need for music industry players and government

to find common ground for partnerships to facilitate industry growth.
- A comprehensive national policy and strategy for the development of the music industry is required.

Conclusions

The development of the Jamaican music industry and the advancement of the business of Reggae within the mainstream music markets of the world, have been stifled by a number of factors both internal and external to Jamaica. Despite the phenomenal accomplishments and worldwide acclaim achieved by Bob Marley, and the unquestionable global appeal of Reggae, the local industry struggles to realize its potential and to secure necessary support to become a major contributor to Jamaica's economy. Within the mainstream popular music markets of the world, several non-Jamaican artists who perform Reggae and Dancehall have had very successful recordings, including UB40, Ace of Bass, Beyonce, Rihanna, Bruno Mars, Jason Mraz, No Doubt, Magic, and Matisyahu.

Apart from Bob Marley, a number of Jamaican artists have been successful at the mainstream popular music level, such as Shaggy, Sean Paul, Shabba Ranks, Diana King, Ini Kamoze, Ziggy and Damian Marley. Despite this, the business of Reggae has not been integrated into the mainstream of the world's largest music markets, such as the USA, Japan, Germany, England, France, Canada, Brazil, and Australia. With the disappearance of the Island Records brand, there is currently no mainstream business representation of recorded Reggae music. New York based VP Records and Miami based Circle House Studios could, with the injection of creative marketing, rise to fill that gap.

In my view the most significant roadblock in the way of the development of the business of Reggae and the Jamaican music industry has been the lack of commitment by the Jamaican government to the design and implementation of a national industrial policy and development strategy for music and the arts and culture sector. Despite the findings of numerous economic studies and recommendations from local and international experts, successive Jamaican governments have failed to treat music and the arts as priority areas for economic and social development. There continues to be an absurd amount of ignorance displayed by various Jamaican ministers of government and their technical advisors with regard to the global impact, relevance and economic potential of Reggae.

Significant local private initiatives aimed at product improvement and marketing such as Reggae Sunsplash, Rebel Salute and Reggae Month, have struggled with inadequate government support or facilitation. Reggae Sunsplash eventually died, and has been replaced by Reggae Sumfest, which in my view is somewhat lacking in its commitment to promote Reggae. At the same time, other music and entertainment initiatives such as Jamaica Carnival and Jamaica Jazz and Blues that focus on the promotion of non-indigenous Jamaican music have been supported and facilitated by government. Reggae Sunsplash, started in 1978, became the model used by several extremely successful European and North American Reggae festivals currently attracting tens of thousands of fans.

The lack of vision of Jamaican government representatives, and their failure to recognize the potential of a business and industry development model that embraces Jamaican musical culture, has handicapped the growth and development of Jamaica in a serious way. Despite clear evidence of grave weaknesses in music business management and marketing capacity, there continues to be inadequate facilities provided for education and training in these areas. There are no comprehensive music and entertainment business training programs in any of the Jamaican tertiary institutions supported and endorsed by the state. The University of the West Indies, University of Technology, and the Edna Manley College for the Visual and Performing Arts, have all fallen short in their arts and entertainment business management programme offerings. As a consequence, the necessary understanding of music business principles does not exist among Jamaican industry practitioners or the technical advisors of government.

Jamaica's unique cultural practices, including the Rastafari movement and its identification with Africa and suffering peoples around the world, have provided an unquestionable driving force for the global popularity of Reggae. This driving force when applied to the international marketing of Reggae also presents a dichotomy. While Rastafari influenced Reggae messages admonishing colonial and post-colonial exploitation, racial discrimination, and the works of puppet "independent" governments, provide fuel for global marketing of Reggae, these messages also result in resistance from those who financially benefit from the status quo of post-colonial economies. In their short sighted view, detractors only see the awakening of the black youths' African consciousness as a threat. Inside Jamaica, many argue that government support for Reggae business development will always be at a low level because artists perform lyrics that speak out against government corruption and mismanagement.

As a predominantly Christian society Jamaica has evolved with a tradition of very strong anti-gay sentiments. There is still a statute in Jamaica that makes sex between males a criminal offense. Very strong anti-gay commentary has been a feature of several songs in the Dancehall sub-genre of Reggae, with some going to the extreme of advocating violence. The pro-gay international lobby against this aspect of Jamaican music has without doubt had a severe impact on the international careers of many Jamaican artists. Many believe the unfortunate stereotyping of Jamaican music and artists as homophobic has posed one of the biggest barriers in recent years to the advancement of Jamaican Reggae in the music markets of North America and Western Europe.

In recent years regulations governing the performance of overseas artists in major markets such as the USA, Canada, and UK have become much more stringent. Requirements for work visa applications and withholding tax regulations applicable to foreigners, now make it much more difficult for Reggae artists to tour. Coupled with this dilemma has been the rise of several home-grown Reggae artists from North America and Europe who are not subject to the same work permit and tax rules.

Having examined the various internal and external roadblocks to the advancement of the business of Jamaican Reggae, I would conclude that there are self-imposed barriers from within the industry and barriers from entities outside the industry, including government. It is my opinion that the ultimate responsibility rests with the people of Jamaica to take remedial steps collectively to increase the level of awareness of the general public with regard to the cultural origins and global value and appreciation for Reggae. A national industrial policy and implementation strategy for music industry development that includes comprehensive programs of education and training in music business management must be an immediate priority. Jamaican decision makers must take into account the value of heritage, traditions, and cultural influence that can bolster and enhance the Island philosophically as well as financially. The Jamaican music industry lessons will also prove to be relevant to many other developing countries trying to establish a viable music industry.

Jamaica and its Music at a Crossroads
– Facebook note, October 7, 2011 [123]

I think we have over studied and over philosophized about the issues related to the development of Jamaican music and the way we do or fail to do business. At the same time we have failed collectively to plan and implement necessary action to develop and sustain an industry. Ignorance, mediocrity and anything goes, have represented the national industry development policy for too long. End result – we reap what we sow.

We will gain nothing from blaming individuals or groups of individuals. We must take collective responsibility and work together to design and implement a long term development plan.

I am reminded of what Marcus Garvey said: "A people without the knowledge of their past history, origin and culture is like a tree without roots". The degeneration witnessed in recent years in Jamaican music and behaviour is symptomatic of what happens to a tree without roots – it dies, or struggles to survive and grow.

SOLUTION – We need to educate and inform our youths about the origins and value of our Jamaican culture, and also train them to be professional managers of our creative output.

WHO ARE WE – Private Sector (investors and corporate entities that interact with and benefit from the music), Government (Ministries and agencies responsible for Education, Culture,

---

123. https://www.facebook.com/notes/lloyd-stanbury/jamaicas-music-at-a-cross-roads/10150857878885355

Information, Industry & Commerce), Music Industry Operators (individual creators, performers, managers and their respective music organizations and trade associations).

Appendices

Appendix I – Global Music Sales

Music markets with total retail value and share of physical, digital records

Ranking	Market	Retail value US $ (millions)	% Change	Physical	Digital	Performance Rights	Synchroniza tion
	Global total	14,966.00	-0.40%	46.00%	46.00%	6.00%	2.00%
1	United States	4,898.30	2.10%	26.00%	71.00%	0.00%	4.00%
2	Japan	2,627.90	-5.50%	78.00%	17.00%	3.00%	1.00%
3	Germany	1,404.80	1.90%	70.00%	22.00%	7.00%	1.00%
4	United Kingdom	1,334.60	-2.80%	41.00%	45.00%	12.00%	2.00%
5	France	842.80	-3.40%	57.00%	27.00%	13.00%	3.00%
6	Australia	376.10	-6.80%	32.00%	56.00%	9.00%	2.00%
7	Canada	342.50	-11.30%	38.00%	53.00%	6.00%	2.00%
8	South Korea	265.80	19.20%	38.00%	58.00%	3.00%	1.00%
9	Brazil	246.50	2.00%	41.00%	37.00%	21.00%	1.00%
10	Italy	235.20	-4.10%	51.00%	33.00%	13.00%	3.00%
11	Netherlands	204.80	2.10%	45.00%	38.00%	16.00%	1.00%
12	Sweden	189.40	1.30%	15.00%	73.00%	10.00%	2.00%
13	Spain	181.10	15.20%	47.00%	35.00%	17.00%	1.00%
14	Mexico	130.30	-1.40%	41.00%	53.00%	4.00%	2.00%
15	Norway	119.90	0.10%	14.00%	72.00%	12.00%	2.00%
16	Austria	114.90	-2.70%	65.00%	22.00%	13.00%	1.00%
17	Belgium	111.20	-5.80%	49.00%	28.00%	22.00%	0.00%
18	Switzerland	108.20	-8.10%	52.00%	38.00%	9.00%	0.00%
19	China	105.20	5.60%	12.00%	87.00%	0.00%	1.00%
20	India	100.20	-10.10%	31.00%	58.00%	8.00%	3.00%

Source: Figures within the table are based on IFPI 2014 annual report.

This table shows the estimated size of the global music industry in terms of sales and contribution to the economy. The International Federation of the Phonographic Industry (IFPI), reports US$15-billion in global physical and digital sales in 2014 including income from performance rights (six percent) and synchronization (two percent).

In 2006, when recorded music sales totaled US$31 billion, the IFPI estimated that the recorded music segment helped to drive "a much broader music industry, worth more than US$130 billion globally" and cited PricewaterhouseCoopers estimates that "music also is one of the leading creative industries driving the media and entertainment sector that is now worth an estimated US$1.4 trillion" and to have reached $1.8 trillion by 2010.

As noted in the section "Laws and the Business of Music in Jamaica" (Chapter 10), Jamaican and Caribbean statistics are hard to come by but it is hoped these figures will help planners to set baselines and targets for reggae's market share.

The table shows figures for the top 20 countries by sales. The subsequent appendices will zoom in on selected features of the UK and USA album and concert markets. The UK market is especially important as it is the platform from which Jamaican ska, rocksteady and Reggae were launched internationally.

Appendix II – Music Value in the UK Economy by GB £ (billions)

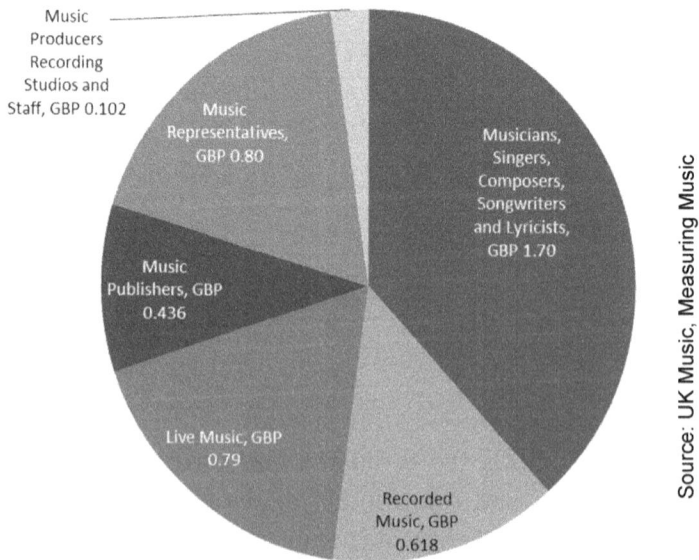

Music Producers Recording Studios and Staff, GBP 0.102

Music Representatives, GBP 0.80

Musicians, Singers, Composers, Songwriters and Lyricists, GBP 1.70

Music Publishers, GBP 0.436

Live Music, GBP 0.79

Recorded Music, GBP 0.618

Source: UK Music, Measuring Music

UK Music's 2014 edition of its annual economic study, Measuring Music, shows that music contributed Gross Value Added (GVA) - of about £3.8bn to the UK economy in 2013. The UK's music attractions including festivals, concert venues and musical heritage sites, generated an estimated £3.1bn of direct and indirect spend in 2014. UK Music is an umbrella organisation representing the collective interests of the UK's commercial music industry, from artists, musicians, songwriters and composers, to major and independent record labels, managers, music publishers, studio producers and collecting societies. Some stats at a glance:

- GVA of £3.8bn
- GVA up 9% year-on-year (£3.5bn in 2012)
- More than 111,000 full time jobs supported
- Music exports of £2.2bn

Appendix III – UK Music Album Sales by Genre

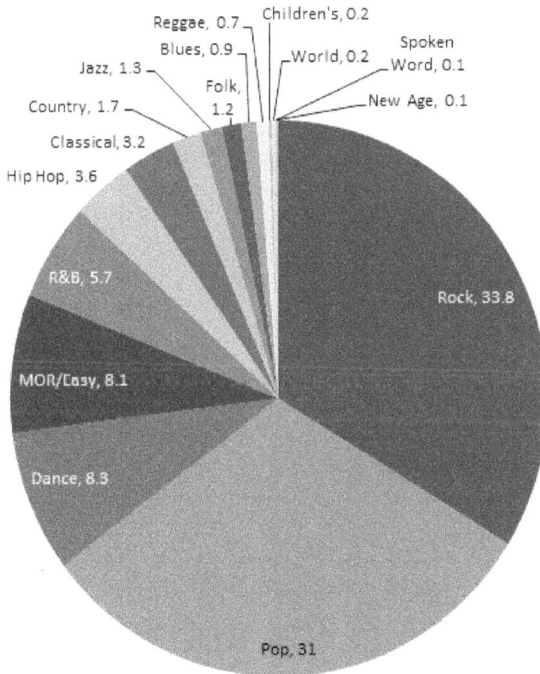

Reggae, 0.7 — Children's, 0.2
Blues, 0.9 — Spoken Word, 0.1
Jazz, 1.3 — World, 0.2
Country, 1.7 — Folk, 1.2
Classical, 3.2 — New Age, 0.1
Hip Hop, 3.6
R&B, 5.7
MOR/Easy, 8.1
Dance, 8.3
Rock, 33.8
Pop, 31

Source: Statista the Statistics Portal

This chart shows the breakdown by genre of UK music album sales in 2013. Rock with 33.8 percent of sales, similar to US market share, was just two points ahead of pop but dwarfed Reggae which, at 0.7 percent, was 12th in a list of 16.

Appendix IV – UK Festival-goers Listening Choice

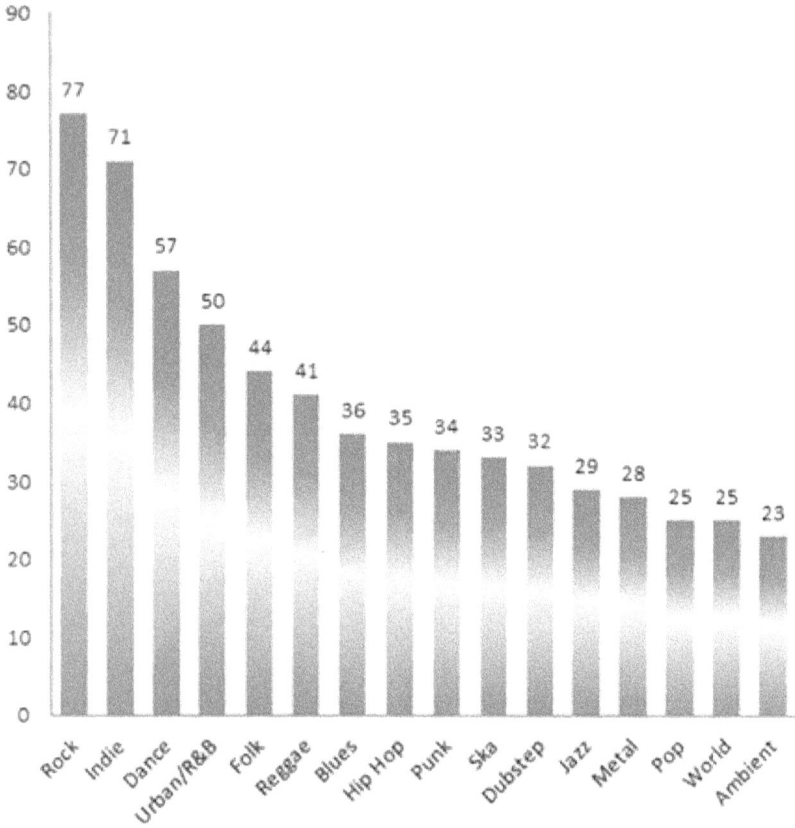

Source: Statista the Statistics Portal

This chart ranks music genres by the share of UK festival-goers who reported listening in 2012. Rock was the most popular at 71 percent of respondents and Reggae was a respectable 6th out of 16 genres with 44 percent of concert-goers reporting listening--the best showing by the genre in comparative statistics.

Appendix V – USA Album Sales by Genre

Rock was the most popular music genre in the USA by album sales in 2013, with 34.8 percent of the market. A note by Statistia, which based its report of data collected by Nielsen Soundscan, says albums may appear in more than one category.

There is no mention of Reggae. Even when Nielsen uses the term 'Other' for a group of genres not listed, it is broken down as a combina-tion of Children's, Christian/Gospel, Classical, Holiday/ Seasonal, Jazz and Latin in addition to less popular genres. Legend – The Best Of Bob Marley And The Wailers, with sales of over 10 million in the US alone up to 2010, is the biggest-selling Reggae album of all-time, according to Guinness World Records.

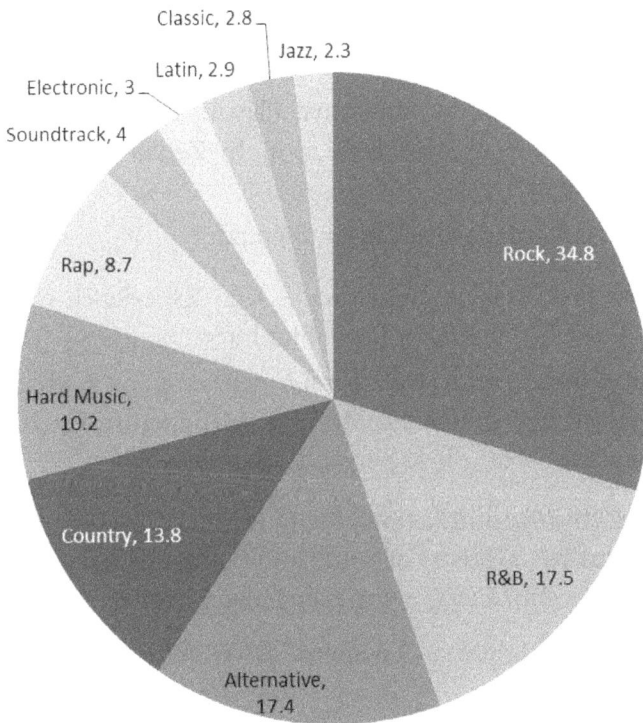

Source: Statista the Statistics Portal

Classic, 2.8
Jazz, 2.3
Latin, 2.9
Electronic, 3
Soundtrack, 4
Rap, 8.7
Hard Music, 10.2
Country, 13.8
Alternative, 17.4
Rock, 34.8
R&B, 17.5

References and Credits

- "Becoming a Globally Competitive Player: The Case of the Music Industry in Jamaica", UNCTAD 1998, by Zeljka Kozul-Wright and Lloyd Stanbury

  http://unctad.org/en/docs/dp_138.en.pdf

- "Mapping the Creative Industries – The Experience of Jamaica", WIPO/CARICOM 2006, by Lloyd Stanbury

  http://www.acpcultures.eu/_upload/ocr_document/ WIPO-CARICOM percent20Meeting_MappingCreativeIndustries_ ExperienceJamaica_Lloyd percent20Stanbury.pdf

- "National Strategy and Action Plan to Further Develop the Jamaican Music Industry", Ministry of Youth and Culture of Jamaica/UNESCO Global Alliance for Culture 2004, by Hillary Brown

- "Music and the Jamaican Economy" UNCTAD/WIPO 2004, by Michael Witter

  http://www.acpcultures.eu/_upload/ocr_document/WIPO_ MusicJamaicanEconomy_2004.pdf

- "Electronic Commerce and Music Business Development in Jamaica: a Portal to the New Economy?" UNCTAD 2002, by Zeljka Kozul Wright, Nicole Foga and Masani Montague – Revised by Mongi Hamdi http://unctad.org/en/docs/iteteb8_en.pdf

- "The Economic Contribution of Copyright-Based Industries in Jamaica", WIPO 2007, by Vanus James

  http://www.wipo.int/export/sites/www/copyright/en/performance/pdf/econ_contribution_cr_ja.pdf

- "Developing Cultural and Creative Industries Policy – The Socio-Politics of Cultural and Creative Industries in the 21st Century: Focus on Jamaica", 2013, by Deborah Hickling

  https://www.academia.edu/6007836/Hickling_1_1_Developing_Cultural_and_Creative_Industries_Policy_The_Socio-Politics_of_Cultural_and_Creative_Industries_in_the_21_st_Century_Focus_on_Jamaica

- "Reggae Routes: The Story of Jamaican Music", 1998, by Kevin O'Brien Chang and Wayne Chen

  http://www.amazon.com/Reggae-Routes-Story-Jamaican-Music/dp/1566396298

- "Profiting from Creativity? The music industry in Stockholm, Sweden and Kingston, Jamaica", 2002, by Dominic Power and Daniel Hallencreutz

  http://www.researchgate.net/publication/23539120_Profiting_from_creativity_The_music_industry_in_Stockholm_Sweden_and_Kingston_Jamaica

- "Prospects for Exports of Entertainment Services from the Caribbean: The Case of Music", 1995, by Compton Bourne and S.M. Allgrove

- "UNESCO 2005 Convention on the Protection and Promotion of the Diversity of Cultural Expressions"

  http://www.unesco.org/new/en/culture/themes/cultural-diversity/diversity-of-cultural-expressions/the-convention/convention-text/

- "UNESCO 1972 Convention Concerning the Protection of the World Cultural and Natural Heritage"

  http://whc.unesco.org/en/conventiontext/

- "Inter_American Commission on Human Rights Annual Report, 2012"

  http://www.oas.org/en/iachr/docs/annual/2012/TOC.asp

- "National Survey of Attitudes and Perceptions of Jamaicans Towards Same Sex Relationships", 2011, University of the West Indies, Mona, Jamaica

  http://www.aidsfreeworld.org/Our-Issues/Homophobia/National-Survey-of-Attitudes-and-Perceptions-of-Jamaicans-Towards-Same-Sex-Relationships.aspx

- "The Ras Tafari Movement in Kingston Jamaica", 1960, by M.G. Smith, Roy Augier, Rex Nettleford

  http://www.cifas.us/sites/g/files/g536796/f/1960e_RasTafariMov_B.pdf , and

  http://www.amazon.com/Report-Rastafari-Movement-Kingston-Jamaica/dp/B001TXGTUC

- "Catch a Fire – The Life of Bob Marley", Revised Edition 2010, by Timothy White

  http://books.google.com/books/about/Catch_A_Fire_The_Life_Of_Bob_Marley.html?id=s8W50pUs1twC

- "Dancehall: From Slave Ship to Ghetto", 2010, by Sonjah Stanley Ni-aah

  http://www.amazon.com/DanceHall-African-Diasporic-Cultural-Studies/dp/0776607367

- "Wake the Town and Tell the People: Dancehall Culture in Jamaica", 2000, by Norman Stolzoff

  http://www.amazon.com/Wake-Town-Tell-People-Dancehall/dp/0822325144

- "The Rough Guide to Reggae", 1997, by Steve Barrow and Peter Dalton

  http://www.amazon.com/Reggae-The-Rough-Guide-Guides/dp/1858282470

- "Sound Clash: Jamaican Dancehall Culture at Large", 2004, by Carolyn Cooper

  http://www.amazon.com/Sound-Clash-Jamaican-Dancehall-Culture/dp/1403964246

- "Inna di Dancehall: Popular Culture and the Politics of Identity in Jamaica", 2000. by Donna P. Hope

  http://www.amazon.com/Inna-Di-Dancehall-Politics-Identity/dp/9766401683

- "Post-Nationalist Geographies: Rasta, Ragga, and Reinventing Africa", 1994, by Louis Chude-Sokei – African Arts – Vol.27

  https://www.amherst.edu/media/view/57455/original/Chude-Sokei, percent20Post-Nationalist percent20Geographies.pdf

- "Stir It Up: The CIA Targets Jamaica, Bob Marley and the Progressive Manley Government", 2012, by David Dusty Cupples

  http://www.amazon.com/Stir-It-Up-Progressive-Government/dp/1477519890

- "Sounding Salsa – Performing Latin Music in New York City", 2008, by Christopher Washburne

  http://www.amazon.com/Sounding-Salsa-Performing-Studies-America/dp/1592133169

- "The Rebel Woman in the British West Indies During Slavery", 1995, by Lucille Mathurin Mair

  http://www.amazon.com/Rebel-British-Indies-During-Slavery/dp/976640206X

- "Rise of Reggaeton", 2010, by Wayne Marshall
  http://norient.com/en/stories/Reggaeton/

- "Know What I mean?: Reflections on Hip Hop", 2010, by Michael Eric Dyson

  http://www.amazon.com/Know-What-Mean-Reflections-Hip-Hop/dp/0465018076

- "40 Years on from the party where Hip Hop was born", 2013, by

Rebecca Lawrence, BBC.

http://www.bbc.com/culture/story/20130809-the-party-where-hip-hop-was-born

- "Can't Stop Won't Stop: A history of the Hip-Hop Generation", 2005, by Jeff Chang

  http://www.amazon.com/Cant-Stop-Wont-History-Generation/dp/0312425791

- "IFPI Digital Music Report 2014"

  http://www.ifpi.org/downloads/Digital-Music-Report-2014.pdf

- "The Future of the Music Business: How to succeed with the New Digital Technologies", 2011, by Steve Gordon

  http://www.amazon.com/The-Future-Music-Business-Technologies/dp/1423499697

- "Roots Rock Reggae: The Oral History of Reggae Music from Ska to Dancehall", 1999, by Chuck Foster

  http://www.amazon.com/Roots-Rock-Reggae-History-Dancehall/dp/0823078310

- "Rastafari – The New Creation" 1997, by Barbara Makeda Blake Hannah

  http://www.amazon.com/Rastafari-Creation-Barbara-Blake-Hannah/dp/9766100470

Author's Biography

Lloyd Stanbury is hailed as a Caribbean pioneer in the field of Entertainment Law. His expertise and experience span a wide range of related activities in the entertainment industry, including the practice of law, artist management, music production, event promotion, research, creative industries policy development, and lecturing.

Mr. Stanbury started his journey in the business of music in 1983 when he organized and presented the Sly and Robbie 10th Anniversary concert in Kingston Jamaica. His impact on the international music scene began in 1990 with his role as co-founder and vice-chairman of the world's first all-Reggae radio station, IRIE-FM, established in Ocho Rios, Jamaica. From 1988 to 1994, Mr. Stanbury had specific responsibility for the station's legal and business affairs, the supervision of its music programming department and the coordination of the IRIE-FM concert series "White River Reggae Bash."

In 1999, Mr. Stanbury established the Caribbean Music Expo (CME), and served as Executive Chairman. Between 1999 and 2004, the CME staged a series of international music business conventions and training workshops, which resulted in participation from hundreds of musicians, music and media business representatives, and organizations from more than 40 countries. Mr. Stanbury has also acted as director and promoter of a number of international live music concert events, including the Reggae Academy Awards staged in Kingston in 2008.

His consultancy services include research and presentations to and on behalf of Jamaican, and international entities, such as the Government of Jamaica; the Caribbean Community (CARICOM) Secretariat; the Caribbean Regional Negotiating Machinery (CRNM); the United Nations Conference on Trade and Development (UNCTAD); the United Nations Educational, Scientific, and Cultural Organization (UNESCO); the Organization of American States (OAS); the World Intellectual Property Organization (WIPO), and Culture et Development in Grenoble, France. His work as a music industry consultant has taken him to South Africa, Kenya, the Seychelles, Senegal, Ivory Coast, Burkina Faso, Trinidad and Tobago, Colombia, Barbados, Dominica, St. Lucia, Guyana, Belize, Cuba, France, Germany, the UK, Canada, and all over the United States of America.

As an entertainment attorney and artist manager, Mr. Stanbury has represented such top artists, music producers, and corporations as Robert Livingston (former manager of Super Cat), Chronixx, Protoje, Assassin a.k.a. Agent Sasco, Half Pint, Freddie McGregor, Steely and Clevie, Da'Ville, Queen Ifrica, Busy Signal, Arrows Recording, Garnett Silk, and Ce'Cile. He has participated in and made presentations at several music business conventions, including MIDEM in Cannes, France; WOMEX in Rotterdam, Holland; A&R Worldwide in Los Angeles; the New Music Seminar and the College Music Journal Conference, both in New York City; the National Association for Campus Activities Conference in Atlanta; the Music and Internet Conference in New York City; South By Southwest in Austin, Texas, and the Black Entertainment and Sports Lawyers Conference in Nassau, Bahamas.

As a champion for structured development within Jamaica's entertainment industry, he has been instrumental in the establishment of a number of music associations and copyright collection societies, including the songwriters agency, Jamaica Association of Composers Authors and Publishers (JACAP); the music producers agency, Jamaica Music Society (JAMMS); and the Recording Industry Association of Jamaica (RIAJam), a trade association that represents corporations in the businesses of production, distribution, and publishing of music.

Mr. Stanbury served as a member of the RIAJam board of directors from 2003 to 2009, and as president of the Jamaica Arts Development Foundation, Inc. He was also an affiliate member of the USA based Association of Arts Administration Educators, and has lectured in law and entertainment management at the University of Technology and the Institute of Management and Production in Jamaica. In 2011 he was selected by UNESCO as a member of its Pool of Experts in the area of culture and governance for developing countries.[124]

Lloyd Stanbury continues to practice as an international music business consultant with offices in Jamaica and South Florida, where he resides.

124.www.unesco.org/new/en/culture/themes/cultural-diversity/2005-convention/technical-assistance/pool-of-experts/stanbury

ISBN 978-0-9867253-7-1

9 780986 725371 >

www.ingramcontent.com/pod-product-compliance
Lightning Source LLC
Chambersburg PA
CBHW051820090426
42736CB00011B/1576

* 9 7 8 0 9 8 6 7 2 5 3 7 1 *